# BEADWORK.
## Creates
# Earrings

# BEADWORK®
## Creates
# Earrings

*Edited by*
*Jean*
*Campbell*

 INTERWEAVE PRESS

Printed and bound in China by Asia Pacific

Editor: Jean Campbell
Copy editor: Christine Townsend
Technical editor: Bonnie Brooks,
                  Jean Campbell
Book design: Paulette Livers
Illustrations: Dustin Wedekind
Photo styling: Paulette Livers
Photography: Joe Coca
Book production: Samantha L. Thaler,
                 Paulette Livers
Proofreader: Nancy Arndt

Library of Congress Cataloging-in-Publication Data

Beadwork creates earrings : 30 designs /
Jean Campbell, editor.
       p. cm.
    ISBN 1-931499-61-6
  1. Beadwork. 2. Earrings. 3. Jewelry making. I.
Campbell, Jean, 1964-
    TT860.B336 2005
    745.594'2--dc22

10 9 8 7 6 5 4 3 2

INTERWEAVE PRESS
201 East Fourth Street
Loveland, Colorado 80537-5655 USA
www.interweave.com

# Dear Reader,

It's easy to get in a rut by wearing the same pair of earrings day in and day out. Don't do it! A great pair of earrings helps draw attention to the most expressive part of the body—your face. Earrings can also be wonderful conversation starters. And once you've got someone looking at your face and talking with you, who knows what can happen?

To avoid the earring rut, Dr. Campbell offers a prescription for 30 fabulous earring projects from top designers. Ranging in technique from simple stringing to challenging off-loom stitching, there's a pair here for every day of the month. And because earrings work up so quickly, there's no excuse for not taking your medicine.

Once you've completed the projects in this book, you'll have a fabulous collection of jewels that include drop, stiletto, stud, chandelier, and hoop shapes. Some earrings are lighthearted for those days when you're feeling that way, others are wild and funky, some are posh and elegant, and still others are downright serious. Whatever mood you're in, you'll have earrings to wear. Most likely they'll complement the necklaces and bracelets already in your jewelry box, or they may inspire you to design pieces that match your new earrings.

As with all the books in our *Beadwork* Creates series, you'll find a useful Techniques section on page 112. It's full of great tips to get you going. It also contains information for those who need to learn new stitches or those whose skills are a little rusty.

So sit down, take some time to relax, and whip up a pair of earrings. You'll feel so much better that you won't need to call me in the morning.

Happy beading!

—Jean Campbell, founding editor, *Beadwork* magazine

*Con*

*nts*

# Holiday Star

*Nikia Angel*

As you'll see when you start making these colorful earrings, you just can't stop making them! Experiment with different colorways in another pair, and, if desired, complete a set at Step 4 for free-standing star shapes. The design is nothing short of magic.

## Materials

Size 15° seed beads
4 faceted 3mm fire-polished glass beads
2 dagger-shaped 10mm glass beads
2 earring wires
Nymo size B beading thread in color to complement beads
Beeswax or synthetic beeswax

## Notions

Size 12 beading needle
Scissors

**Step 1:** Using 3' (91.5 cm) of waxed thread and leaving a 4" (10 cm) tail, string 10 seed beads. Pass through all the beads again to make a foundation circle and exit from the last bead strung. Snug the beads and tie a square knot to secure them. Pass through 2 beads on the circle and pull tight to hide the knot.

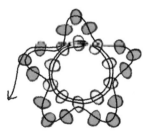

Figure 1

**Step 2:** *String 3 seed beads, skip 1 bead on the foundation circle, and pass through the next bead (Figure 1). Repeat from * around the circle to make five points. Exit from the second bead added in this round.

**Step 3:** *String 5 seed beads and pass through the second bead of the next point. Repeat from * around the circle to make five points (Figure 2). Pass through the first and second bead added in this round.

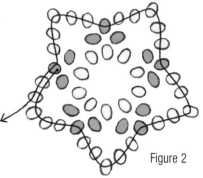

Figure 2

**Step 4:** String 3 seed beads and pass through the fourth and fifth beads of the first point made in Step 3. Follow the existing thread path so you exit from the second bead of the next point. Continue around the circle, adding three seed beads to each point created in Step 3 (Figure 3). Pass through the first three beads added in this round.

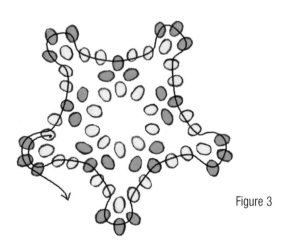

Figure 3

**Step 5:** *String 5 seed beads and pass through the next three beads added in Step 4. Repeat from * around until you've connected the five points. Pass through the first and second bead added in this round.

**Step 6:** *String 3 seed beads and pass through the fourth and fifth beads added in Step 5 and the first bead of the next point created in Step 4. String 3 beads and pass through the third bead of the same point created in Step 4 and the first and second beads added in the next point from Step 5 (Figure 4). Repeat from * around the circle to make ten picots. Exit from the second bead added in this round.

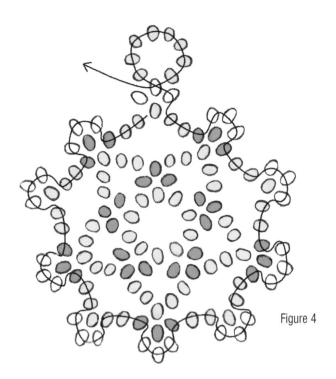

Figure 4

**Step 7:** String 8 seed beads and pass through the bead you just exited (Figure 4). Pass through all the beads again to reinforce the loop.

**Step 8:** Weave through the beadwork and exit from the picot opposite the loop made in Step 7. String 3 seed beads, 1 fire-polished bead, 5 seed beads, 1 dagger, and 2 seed beads. Pass back through the third seed bead of the 5-seed bead segment and up through the other beads on the fringe leg.

**Step 9:** Weave through all the beads in the earring to secure and trim close to the work. Add an earring wire to the top loop.

**Step 10:** Repeat Steps 1–9 to make the second earring.

*Nikia Angel spends her days in Albuquerque surrounded by beads as she makes kits to lure unsuspecting folks into the beading world. She is co-owner of www.BuytheKit.com.*

# Confetti Hoops

*Joanie Jenniges*

Weave tiny bits of color into a hoop to celebrate your favorite focal bead then let the compliments begin when you put them on!

## Materials

- Size 11° Japanese seed beads
- Size 14° Japanese seed beads
- 2 round or faceted 5mm Swarovski pearls, semi-precious stone or Czech fire-polished beads
- 4 silver, gold, or glass 4mm heishe beads
- 2 sterling silver or gold-filled earring wires
- Size D Nymo in color to complement beads
- Beeswax or synthetic beeswax

## Notions

- Size 12 beading needle
- Scissors
- Chain-nose pliers

**Step 1:** Using 1 yd (91.5 cm) of thread and leaving a 6" (15 cm) tail, string 4 size 11°s, 1 heishe, one 5mm, 1 heishe, and 21 size 11°s. Note: Be sure that the size 11°s on either side of the heishe beads have large enough holes to accommodate numerous thread passes. Use a square or surgeon's knot to tie all the beads in a circle. Pass through the first 8 beads.

**Step 2:** String 2 size 11°s and 9 size 14°s. Pass through the fourth and fifth size 14°s strung in this

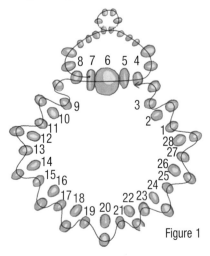

Figure 1

step to make a small circle. String 3 size 14°s and 2 size 11°s. Pass through the fourth through eighth beads strung in Step 1 (Beads 4–8, Figure 1).

**Step 3:** String 1 size 11°. Pass through Bead 9. String 1 size 11° and pass through Bead 11. Continue stringing 1 size 11°, skipping a size 11° in the original circle and passing through the next size 11° in the circle until you've strung 13 size 11°s in this step. Pass through Beads 4–8 and the first size 11° strung in this step.

**Step 4:** *String 1 size 11° and pass through the next size 11° strung in Step 3. Repeat from * until you've added a total of 12 size 11°s in this step. Pass through the fourth through eighth beads strung in Step 1. *Note:* You may need to string more than one bead at certain points to fill gaps or to hide exposed thread. If you do so, make sure to keep the bead count the same on both sides of the circle.

**Step 5:** Weave through all beads to secure, strengthen, and enhance the beadwork's circular shape. Secure working and tail threads, tying half-hitch knots between beads if desired. Trim threads close to work.

**Step 6:** Using the chain-nose pliers, carefully attach the ear wires to the size 14° loop at the top of the beadwork.

**Step 7:** Repeat Steps 1 through 6 for the second earring.

---

*With the support of her husband and four children, Minnesotan Joanie Jenniges shares her passion for beadwork through designing and teaching. She can be reached at joaniejenniges@comcast.net or www.beadworkdesigns.com.*

**VARIATION**
For a ruffled look, string 2 size 11°s each time in Step 4 before you pass through the previously placed beads in Step 3.

# Crystal Tassels

*Nancy Zellers*

These spectacular earrings make a regal addition to your jewelry collection. With a rich combination of ruby-, emerald-, and sapphire-colored crystals, they're fit for a queen.

## Materials

- 6 g of size 15° silver-lined gold seed beads
- 12 bicone 4mm Siam Swarovski crystals
- 12 bicone 4mm emerald Swarovski crystals
- 12 bicone 4mm cobalt Swarovski crystals
- 2 round 4mm gold-plated beads
- 2 round 3mm gold-plated beads
- 2 gold earring wires
- Size D gold Nymo beading thread
- Thread conditioner

## Notions

- Size 12 beading needle
- Scissors

**Step 1:** Condition a 3' (91.5 cm) length of thread. Work a strip of right-angle weave 5 units long. Use the crystals to form the bottom of the right-angle weave units and 2 seed beads to form the sides. See Figure 1 for the crystal color placement.

**Step 2:** Continue working right-angle weave until the beadwork is 5 units long by 3 units wide. See Figure 2 for crystal color placement.

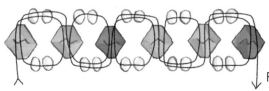

Figure 1

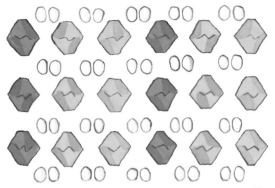

Figure 2

**Step 3:** Fold the bead strip so short sides meet. Use seed beads to make a final right-angle weave stitch and connect the ends (Figure 3). Doing so will form a short tube.

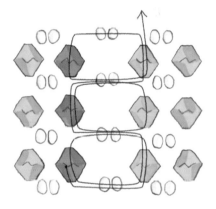

Figure 3

**Step 4:** Pass through one pair of seed beads on the outer edge of the tube. *String 1 seed bead and pass through the pair of seed beads. Repeat from * around the tube's edge, keeping the beads snug.

**Step 5:** Make a simple fringe of seed beads from each of the seed beads at the edge of this end of the tube. Begin by exiting an edge bead. String 33 seed beads and, skipping the last bead strung, pass back through 32. Pass back through the bead you initially exited and through the next edge bead (Figure 4). Continue to make fringe legs around the edge of the tube for a total of 18 fringes.

**Step 6:** Weave the thread to the opposite edge of the tube and repeat Step 4.

**Step 7:** Create a domed cap of seed beads with tubular peyote stitch. You will work from the round of seed beads at the edge of the tube.

**Rounds 1 and 2:** *String 1 seed bead, skip a bead at the edge of the tube, and pass through the next one. Repeat from * for a total of 9 beads. Exit from the first bead added in this round.

**Round 3:** Make two decreases in this round to add a total of 7 beads. Space the two decreases across from one another.

**Round 4:** Work this round to add a total of 7 beads.

**Round 5:** Make two decreases in this round to add a total of 5 beads. Space the two decreases across from one another.

**Round 6:** Work this round to add a total of 5 beads. Pass through all the beads just added and pull tightly.

Figure 4

**Step 8:** String 3 seed beads, one 4mm gold round, and 3 seed beads. Pass through a seed bead on the opposite side of the ring of beads created in Step 7, Round 6. Pass through all these beads again to reinforce. Exit from the gold round.

**Step 9:** String 3 seed beads, one 3mm gold round, and 3 seed beads. Pass back through the 3mm and 4mm gold round beads. Pass through all these beads again to reinforce. Exit from the 3mm gold round.

**Step 10:** String 6 seed beads and pass through the 3mm gold round bead. Pass through all these beads again to reinforce.

**Step 11:** Weave the working and tail threads into the beadwork. Tie knots between beads, if desired, pass through several more beads, and trim close to the work. Attach an earring wire to the loop at the top of the dome cap.

**Step 12:** Repeat Steps 1–11 for the second earring.

---

*Nancy Zellers likes simple but elegant jewelry projects. Kits are available for some of her designs. Contact her at nzbeads@aol.com.*

# Sweet Violets

*SaraBeth Cullinan*

No matter what the season, these delightful square-stitched earrings will keep spring in your heart—or, at the very least, on your ears.

## Materials

- 3 g each of lavender and purple Delicas
- 1 g yellow Delicas
- Size B Nymo thread in color to complement the main color beads
- 2 sterling silver earring posts
- 6" (15 cm) chain
- 6 jump rings

## Notions

- Size 12 beading needles
- Scissors
- Pliers
- Wire cutters

**Step 1,** Row 1: Add a tension bead halfway down a 6' (183 cm) length of the thread. Follow the chart on page 21, starting with the row marked with a red star. String the beads for the row.
Row 2: String the first bead indicated for the second row on the chart, pass through the bead directly below it, and back through the bead just strung. Repeat to the end of the row. Pass through both Row 1 and this row to reinforce each. Exit from the bead below the point at which the next row begins.
Rows 3–5 (decrease rows): Follow the chart, working these rows in square stitch.
Rows 6 and 7 (increase rows): Follow the chart from black dot to black dot. After finishing Row 7, string 2 beads and weave down into the first bead of Row 6, up through the bead directly above it, into the top

**19**

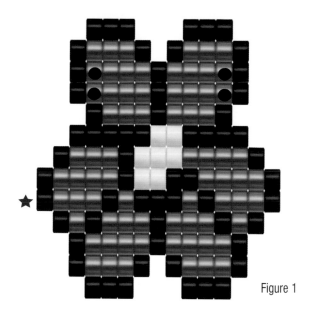

Figure 1

increasing bead, then down into Row 6, exiting the opposite side of the piece. String 2 beads and weave up into the first bead of Row 7, down through the bead that is directly below it, into the bottom increasing bead, and up into Row 7, exiting the other side of the piece.

**Rows 8 and 9 (petals):** Follow the chart to finish one side of Rows 8 and 9. Weave down into Row 7 and exit the opposite side of the piece and finish the other petal. Weave through all the beads in the body of the earring to reinforce and trim the thread.

**Step 2:** Remove the tension bead and use the remaining thread to finish the bottom of the earring. Use the decrease techniques detailed in Step 1 to complete the petals below the starred row of the pattern. When you're finished, add an 8-bead loop to the corner of a petal and weave through the loop several times to reinforce it. Weave through all the beads in the body of the earring for reinforcement and trim the thread close to the work.

**Step 3:** Repeat Steps 1 and 2 to make a second violet.

**Step 4:** After making 2 violets, cut 1 piece of chain ⅜" (1 cm) long and 1 piece 1" (2.5 cm) long. Use jump rings to attach the cut chain to each violet through the 8-bead loops. Pair the chains together and connect them with a jump ring at the loose end. Attach the chained violets to the earring finding with the jump ring.

**Step 5:** Repeat Steps 1–4 to make a second earring.

---

*When SaraBeth Cullinan isn't working for beads at one of the many bead shows across the country, she is at home in sunny Arizona where she beads and belly dances. She can be reached at sarabeth44@msn.com.*

# Druid Dangles

*Nikki Blanchard*

This willowy earring design is created with custom-made resin pieces. It can also be made with horizontally-drilled glass leaves and bell flowers. Either way, the earrings make a great excuse to become adorned with flowers!

## Materials

- 2 vertically drilled 12mm × 20mm leaf-shaped resin beads
- 2 bell flower 10mm resin beads
- 2 bicone 3mm Swarovski crystals
- 2 bicone 4mm Swarovski crystals
- 4 sterling silver 3" (7.5 cm) eye pins
- 2 sterling silver 2" head pins with 2 mm round head
- 2 sterling silver earring wires

## Notions

- Round-nose pliers
- Chain-nose pliers
- Wire cutters

**Step 1:** Use an eye pin to string 1 leaf bead and one 4mm crystal at the point of the leaf. Make a wrapped loop. Set aside.

**Step 2:** Use an eye pin to string 1 flower bead from inside the bell to the outside. To secure the bead, make a wrapped loop that captures the bottom loop of Step 1's dangle.

**Step 3:** Use a head pin to string one 3mm crystal. To secure the bead, make a wrapped loop that captures the loop inside the flower.

**Step 4:** Repeat Steps 1–3 to make a second earring.

*Nikki Blanchard is the proprietor of The Moontide Workshop, www.moontideworkshop.com.*

# Watermelon Balls

*Anna Tollin*

Watermelon tourmaline is a beautiful semiprecious stone that has a range of green, white, and red shades. Instead of actual tourmaline, however, these clever earrings feature bicone crystals in an array of those same shades. The crystals successfully mimic the stone, and they're much easier to find.

## Materials

8 bicone 4mm satin jonquil Swarovski crystals
8 bicone 4mm satin light rose Swarovski crystals
8 bicone 4mm satin peridot Swarovski crystals
2 bicone 4mm clear fuchsia Swarovski crystals
2 bicone 4mm green tourmaline Swarovski crystals
2 thin sterling silver 2" head pins
2 sterling silver earring wires
24" (61 cm) of Illusion cord

## Notions

Scissors
Round-nose pliers
Chain-nose pliers
Side cutter

**Step 1:** Cut 12" (30.5 cm) of cord and hold both ends, one in each hand. String 1 jonquil crystal and slide it to the middle of the cord.

**Step 2:** Use the left cord end to string 1 light rose crystal and 1 jonquil crystal. Use the right cord to string 1 peridot crystal and pass back through (cross through) the jonquil crystal last strung so the cord crosses within that bead (Figure 1). Doing so will create a diamond shape with the beads.

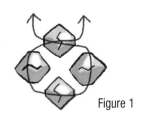

Figure 1

**25**

**Step 3:** Repeat Step 2 until you've woven 12 crystals in all. End by crossing through the first jonquil crystal strung in Step 1. Now you have created a circle of beads.

**Step 4:** Tie a half hitch knot between beads and pass through another to hide the knot. Make three more knots with each cord end to secure the beads. Trim the cord close to the work. Set aside.

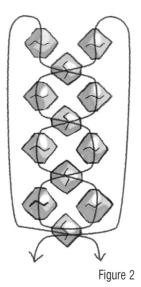

Figure 2

**Step 5:** Use a head pin to string 1 fuchsia crystal, the beadwork completed in Step 3, and 1 green tourmaline crystal. Make a wrapped loop to secure the beads. Attach the dangle to an earring wire.

**Step 6:** Repeat Steps 1–5 to make a second earring.

---

*Anna Tollin left corporate America to pursue a more creative and authentic life. She works at The Bead Monkey in Minneapolis and will do almost anything for chocolate!*

# At the Carwash

*Jamie Hogsett*

These swishing dangly earrings are easier to make than they look. But you won't have to close your car windows when you wear them!

## Materials

40 size 11° purple Japanese seed beads
600 size 11° green Japanese seed beads
2 sterling silver French earring wires
28" (71 cm) of 22-gauge sterling silver wire
56" (142 cm) of Fireline 6 lb test line

## Notions

Size 12 beading needle
Wire cutters
Flat-nose pliers
Round-nose pliers

**Step 1:** Make a wrapped loop on the end of a 3" (7.5 cm) piece of wire. String 3 purple. Make a wrapped loop on the other end to secure the beads. Attach one end to an earring wire.

**Step 2:** Make a double simple loop on the end of a 3" (7.5 cm) piece of wire. String 4 purple, the piece made in Step 1, and 4 purple. Make a double simple loop on the other end of the wire.

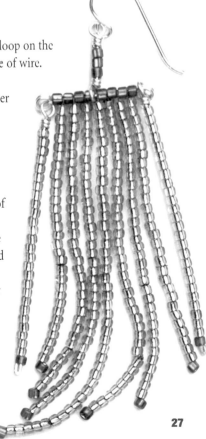

27

**Step 3:** Using flat-nose pliers, bend the last ⅛" (3 mm) of a 4" (10 cm) piece of wire back onto itself. String 1 purple and 26 green. Use a wrapped loop to connect this piece to one end of the piece made in Step 2. Repeat this step for the other end of the piece made in Step 2.

**Step 4:** Using a square knot, attach a 4" (10 cm) piece of Fireline to the middle of the piece from Step 2. String 42 green and 1 purple. Pass back through 8–16 purple and tie a small overhand knot. Continue passing up through the beads to hide the knot. Trim the thread close to the work.

**Step 5:** Repeat Step 4 three times on each side of the strand made in Step 4, decreasing by 4 green seed beads each time as you move away from the middle strand (38, 34, 30).

**Step 6:** Repeat Steps 1–5 to make a second earring.

---

*Jamie Hogsett is projects editor for Beadwork magazine.*

# Retro Wraps

*Jennifer Sevlie Diederich*

This spirited look from the 1960s and 1970s is made new again with up-to-date color choices. By wrapping the large drop with an assortment of beads on wire you'll make your own statement.

## Materials

2 top-drilled 15mm × 40mm elongated drop beads
Size 6°, 8°, and 11° seed beads to complement the top-drilled beads
4mm bicone cut crystals or triangles
2 earring wires
24" (61 cm) of 26-gauge wire

## Notions

Round-nose pliers
Side cutter

**Step 1:** Cut a 12" (30.5 cm) piece of wire and insert it through a top-drilled bead from left to right, leaving about 3" (7.5 cm) on the right side.

**Step 2:** Bend the right-side wire up and around the top of the bead. Bend the left-side wire up and around the top of the bead and straight up to form a spine for a wire bail.

**Step 3:** Wrap the right-side wire around the spine three times. Trim with the side cutter (Figure 1).

Figure 1

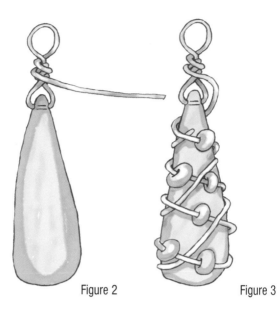

Figure 2                  Figure 3

**Step 4:** Use a round-nose pliers to make a loop with the spine wire. Wrap this wire down the spine to meet the existing wire wrap (Figure 2).

**Step 5:** String an assortment of beads on the remaining wire. Move a few beads toward the large bead and wrap the wire around it. Continue moving a few beads toward the large bead and wrapping the wire randomly around it until you have 3" (7.5 cm) of wire left. Weave the remaining wire back up through the beads to hold them in place and hide the wire end. Trim the wire when you reach the top of the large bead (Figure 3).

**Step 6:** Open the loop on the ear wire and place the earring through the loop and close.

**Step 7:** Repeat Steps 1 through 6 to make the second earring.

---

*Jennifer Sevlie Diederich has been working and teaching at The Bead Monkey in St. Paul, Minnesota, for the past four years, and she loves being surrounded by so many creative people, ideas, and BEADS.*

# Chained Reflection

*Joanie Jenniges*

These earrings are simple, chic, and fun, and they take advantage of the earring post—a jewelry finding that's often ignored. Try the suggested earrings here or experiment with your own color combinations and a variety of crystal shapes and sizes.

## Materials

- 4 tanzanite 6mm Swarovski cube crystals
- 4 tanzanite 4mm Swarovski cube crystals
- 8 black diamond 2X AB 4mm Swarovski bicone crystals
- 4 medium sterling silver 1" (2.5 cm) head pins (.25 to .28 thick)
- 12 medium sterling silver 1" (2.5 cm) eye pins (.25 to .28 thick)
- 2 sterling silver 4mm earring ball posts with loops and winged ear nut backings
- 2 sterling silver 5.5mm jump rings
- 33-link length of sterling silver 2.2 mm flat cable chain

## Notions

- Chain-nose pliers
- Round-nose pliers
- Flush cutters

**Step 1:** Cut the chain into pieces, three pieces with two links each and four pieces with one link each.

**Step 2:** String one 6mm cube on a head pin and make a simple loop close to the cube. Trim the extra wire. Repeat with another 6mm cube to make 2 dangles.

**Step 3:** String one 4mm cube on an eye pin and make a simple

Variation

loop close to the cube. Trim the extra wire. Repeat with the 3 remaining 4mm cubes to make 4 links.

**Step 4:** String 1 bicone on an eye pin and make a simple loop close to the cube. Trim the extra wire. Repeat with the 7 remaining bicones to make 8 links.

**Step 5:** Open the loop on the ball post, string a two-link piece of chain, and close the loop. Attach a bicone link to the end of the chain. Attach a two-link chain piece to the end of the bicone link. Attach a bicone link to the end of the chain. Attach a one link chain piece to the end of the bicone link. Attach a 4mm cube link to the end of the chain. Attach a two-link chain piece to the end of the cube link. Attach the 6mm cube dangle to the end of the chain.

Figure 1

**Step 6:** Open a jump ring and attach it to one of the loops of the earring nut; close the jump ring. Attach a bicone link to the jump ring. Attach a one-link chain piece to the end of the bicone link. Attach a cube link to the end of the chain. Attach a one-link chain piece to the end of the cube link. Attach a bicone link to the end of the chain. Attach a one-link chain piece to the end of the bicone link. Attach a cube dangle to the end of the chain.

**Step 7:** Repeat Steps 1–6 to make a second earring.

*With the support of her husband and four children, Minnesotan Joanie Jenniges shares her passion for beadwork through designing and teaching. She can be reached at joaniejenniges@comcast.net or www.beadworkdesigns.com.*

# Tier Drops

*Dustin Wedekind*

It's inevitable to have beads left over from any bracelet or necklace project. If you've got drop beads in your cast-offs, this simple design is a swinging way to use them up and make a matching ensemble.

## Materials

Size 15° seed beads
2 top-drilled ½"–1" (1.3–2.5 cm) drop beads
2–6 rondelle 8mm–10mm beads
2 sterling silver or gold-filled French earring wires
10 lb test PowerPro beading thread

## Notions

Size 10 beading needle
Scissors
Flat-nose pliers
Lighter (optional)

**Step 1:** Using 14" (35.5 cm) of thread and leaving a 4" (10 cm) tail, string 7 seed beads and pass through the first 6 again to form a circle.

**Step 2:** String 5–7 seed beads and 1 rondelle. *String 3 seed beads and 1 rondelle. Repeat from * for the desired number of rondelles.

**Step 3:** String 5 or more seed beads. These beads should measure from the top of the drop bead to the hole. Pass through the drop and string the same number of seed beads already added in this step. Pass back through the last rondelle (Figure 1).

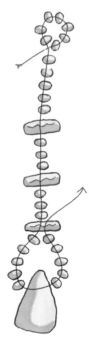

Figure 1

**Step 4:** *String 3 seed beads and pass back through the next rondelle. Repeat from * until you reach the last rondelle. String 5–7 seed beads to reach the initial circle of beads created in Step 1. Exit from the bead that includes the tail thread.

**Step 5:** Tie a square knot with the working and tail threads, being sure that the beads are snug. Pass back through the seventh bead of the circle and down a few beads of the first leg. Thread the needle onto the tail thread and pass it back through a few beads of the second leg. Trim both threads close to the work; if necessary, use a lighter to carefully melt the ends.

**Step 6:** Use the pliers to twist the ear wire loop open. Place the circle of beads in the loop, and then twist the wire back in place.

**Step 7:** Repeat Steps 1–6 to make a second earring.

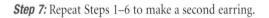

*Dustin Wedekind is the senior editor of* Beadwork *magazine and can wear four earrings in each ear. Bling. Bling.*

# Crystal Extravaganza

*Melody MacDuffee*

The designer, a former tomboy, says she hasn't always been at ease with froufrou styles in her clothing and jewelry. But these earrings gave her the freedom to be as outrageous, glitzy, and uninhibited as she dared to be.

## Materials

- 2 g size 11° gold silver-lined Japanese seed beads
- 8 round 6mm pink AB Swarovski crystals
- 6 flattened round 6mm pale gold AB Swarovski crystals
- 10 bicone 6mm dark green AB Swarovski crystals
- 8 vertically-drilled teardrop 6 × 10 pink AB Swarovski crystals
- 42 bicone 4mm pink AB Swarovski crystals
- 12 bicone 4mm light green AB Swarovski crystals
- 10 bicone 4mm dark green AB Swarovski crystals
- 10 bicone 6mm dark green AB Swarovski crystals
- 14 bicone 3mm light green 3mm Swarovski crystals
- 16 gold-filled head pins
- 2½ yd (228.5 cm) of 24-gauge gold-filled wire
- 1' (30.5 cm) of 22-gauge gold-filled wire
- 2' (61. cm) of fine gauge gold-filled chain
- 2 soldered 4 mm gold-filled jump rings
- 2 gold-filled earring wires

## Notions

Flat-nose pliers
Round-nose pliers
Wire cutters

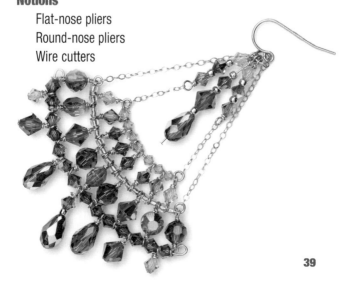

**Step 1:** Use the 24-gauge wire to make 1-bead wire-wrapped connectors (a loop on each side of the bead) for each of the following beads: 4 light green 4mm bicones, 4 dark green 4mm bicones, 8 pink 4mm bicones, 8 pink 6mm rounds, 6 pale gold flattened 6mm rounds, and 4 dark green 6mm bicones. Set the 34 connectors aside.

**Step 2:** Use head pins to make 1-bead wire-wrapped dangles for each of the following beads: 4 light green 4mm bicones, 4 dark green 6mm bicones, and 4 pink teardrops.

*Use a head pin to string 1 pink teardrop, 1 size 11°, and a dark green 4mm bicone. Make a wrapped loop to secure. Repeat from * to make a second long dangle. Set all 14 dangles aside.

**Step 3:** Cut four ⅝" (1.5 cm) lengths of chain and four 2⅝" (6.6 cm) lengths. Set the 8 pieces of chain aside.

**Step 4:** Cut two 1½" (3.8 cm) lengths of 22-gauge wire, two 2½" (6.5 cm) lengths, and two 3½" (9 cm) lengths. Use the round-nose pliers to make a simple loop on one end of each wire.

**Step 5:** Use one of the 1½" (3.8 cm) lengths of wire to string the following connectors with 1 light green 3mm bicone between each: 1 light green 4mm bicone, 1 dark green 4mm bicone, 4 pink 4mm bicones, 1 dark green 4mm bicone, and 1 light green 4mm bicone. Make a simple loop at the end of the wire to secure the connectors and beads. If the beads don't fit snugly on the wire, uncurl the loop, cut off the excess wire, and make another loop.

**Step 6:** Use one of the 2½" (6.5 cm) lengths of 22-gauge wire to string 1 pink 6mm round. *String 1 size 11°, 1 single link of chain, the bottom loop of the first (next) 4mm bicone from Step 5, a single link of chain, 1 size 11°, 1 single link of chain, and 1 flattened 6mm round. Repeat from *, substituting the following connectors (in order) for the flattened 6mm round: 1 dark green 6mm bicone; 1 pink 6mm round; 1 flattened 6mm round; 1 pink 6mm round; 1 dark green 6mm bicone; 1 flattened 6mm round; 1 pink 6mm round. Make a simple loop at the end of the wire to secure the beads.

**Step 7:** Use one of the 3½" (9 cm) lengths of 22-gauge wire to string the bottom loop of the first connector from Step 6, 1 pink 4mm bicone, 1 light green 4mm bicone connector, 1 pink 4mm bicone, the bottom loop of the next connector from Step 6, and 1 pink 4mm bicone, 1 light green 6mm bicone connector. String 1 pink 4mm bicone, the bottom loop of the next connector from Step 6, 1 pink 4mm bicone, 1 short teardrop dangle, 1 pink 4mm bicone, the bottom loop of the next connector from Step 6, 1 pink 4mm bicone, the long teardrop dangle, and the next connector from Step 6. Repeat the stringing sequence for this step in reverse, omitting the long teardrop dangle. Make a simple loop at the end of the wire to secure the beads.

**Step 8:** *Use a 2" (5 cm) length of 24-gauge wire to make a wrapped loop that captures a jump ring in the loop. String 1 light green 4mm bicone, 1 size 11°, 1 pink 4mm bicone, 1 size 11°, and 1 dark green 4mm bicone. Make a wrapped loop with the other end of the wire that captures the end of a ⅝" (1.5 cm) length of chain in the loop. Repeat from * once using the same soldered jump ring.

**Step 9:** Open one side loop on the top crossbar of the earring and attach the end link of the chain added in Step 8. Repeat for the second chain. Close the loop securely when you are finished.

**Step 10:** Attach one end of a 2¼" (5.5 cm) length of chain to each side loop on the second crossbar of the earring and close the loops securely when you are finished.

**Step 11:** Making sure that the jump rings are at the front of the earring, attach the earring wire to the jump ring, hooking the top link of the long chains into the earring wire loop as well. You may have to adjust the length of the chains so that the earring hangs at the length desired. If you hook the right-hand chain in first and the left-hand one second for the first earring, do the opposite for the second earring, so that their natural swing is in opposite directions and allows them to lie nicely alongside the face.

**Step 12:** Use a head pin to string 1 pink teardrop, 1 size 11°, 1 dark green 6mm biconc, 1 size 11°, 1 pink 4mm bicone, and 1 size 11°. Leaving about ½" (1.3 cm) of wire exposed at the top, make a wrapped loop that captures the jump ring between the two short chains.

**Step 13:** Repeat Steps 5–12 to make the other earring.

---

*Melody MacDuffee has been making jewelry for many years, at first exclusively with crochet, and then gradually expanding her love of her tiny hooks and beads to a love of equally tiny beading needles and lengths of wire. She is widely published in bead and crochet publications and teaches a variety of techniques in her classes.*

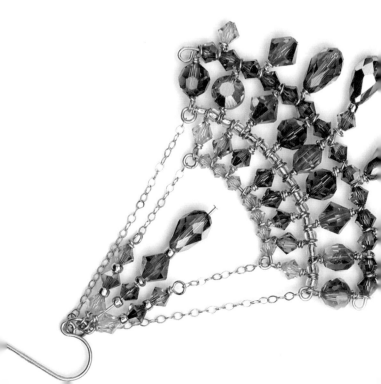

# Crystal Elegance

*Joanie Jenniges*

Experimenting with moss stitch produced this pretty double-sided, three-dimensional design that employs Swarovski crystals. With or without the drops, they work up quickly.

## Materials

Size 11° Japanese seed beads
Size 14° Japanese seed beads
8 semiprecious stone 3 × 5 tube beads
16–21 bicone 4mm Swarovski crystals
2 bicone 6mm Swarovski crystals
2 sterling silver or gold-filled earring wires
2 sterling silver or gold-filled 1½" (3.8 cm) head pins
  (.25 to .28 thick)
5' (152.5 cm) size B Fireline (4 lb test, extra fine) or size
  B Nymo
Beeswax or synthetic beeswax

## Notions

Size 12 beading needle
Scissors
Round-nose pliers
Chain-nose pliers
Wire cutters

**Step 1:** Using 2½' (76 cm) of thread and leaving a 12" tail, string four tubes (Beads 1–4). Use a square knot to tie them together to make a diamond shape. Pass through all the tubes again, exiting from Bead 4 so that the working thread, tail thread, and knot are all between the first and fourth tubes. Consider the corners of the diamond as a compass, with a North, South, East, and West.

**Step 2:** String 1 size 11° and pass through Bead 1. String 1 size 11° and pass through Bead 2. String 1 size 11° and pass through Bead 3. String 1 size 11° and pass through Bead 4.

Exit from the first bead added in this step (Figure 1).

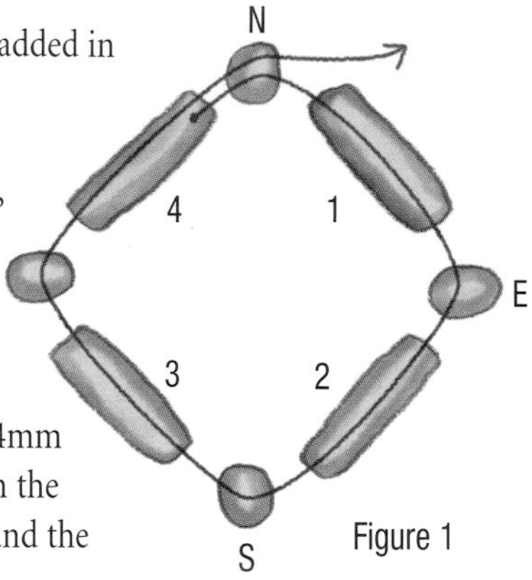

**Step 3:** String one 4mm, 1 size 11°, and one 4mm. Pass through the West size 11°. Pass back through the last 4mm, size 11°, and 4mm just strung. Pass through the North size 11°, Bead 1, and the East size 11°.

Figure 1

**Step 4:** String one 4mm. Pass through the size 11° strung in Step 3 (doing so will seat the size 11° at the center of the diamond). String one 4mm. Pass through the South size 11°. Pass back through the last 4mm, the size 11° at the center of the diamond, and the first 4mm just strung. Pass through the East size 11°, Bead 2, and the South size 11° (Figure 2).

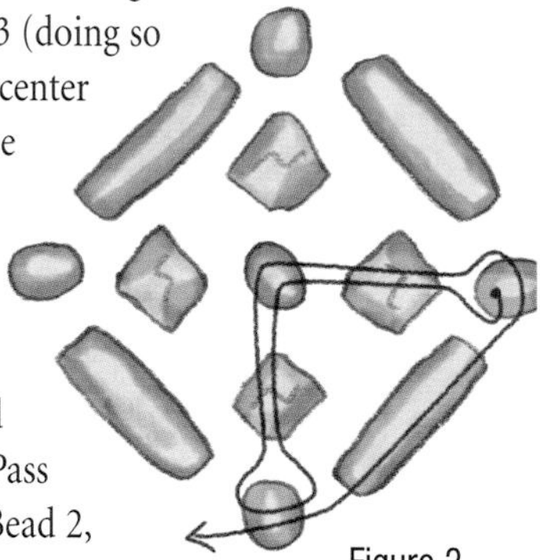

Figure 2

**Step 5:** Work the back of the earring. Repeat Steps 3 and 4, keeping in mind that the East and West size 11°s, Beads 1 and 4, and Beads 2 and 3 are now in reversed positions. Turn the work over to the front.

**Step 6:** If you wish to add drops, string 6 size 14°s. Pass through the South size 11° and all the beads strung in this step. Pass through the South size 11°, Bead 3, the West size 11°, Bead 4, the North size 11°, Bead 1, the East size 11°, and Bead 2. Pass back through the beads added in this step (in a clockwise direction). Pass through Bead 3 (Figure 3).

**Step 7:** Weave the working thread through the beadwork to

reinforce and secure. Tie a knot between beads and pass through a few more to hide the knot. Trim the thread close to the work.

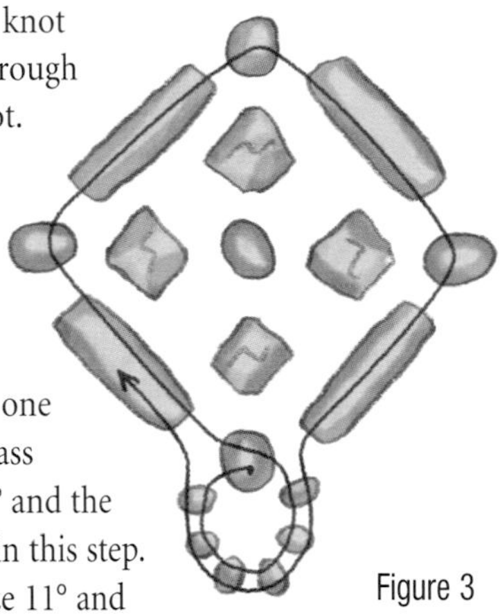

Figure 3

**Step 8:** Use the tail thread to pass through the North size 11°. String 3 size 14°s, one ear wire, and 3 size 14°s. Pass through the North size 11° and the beads and ear wire added in this step. Pass through the North size 11° and Bead 1. Weave the tail thread through the beadwork, tie a knot between beads, and pass through a few beads to hide the knot. Trim the thread close to the work.

**Step 9:** If you've set up your beadwork for a drop (Step 6), string 1 size 11°, one 6mm, and 1 size 11° on a head pin. Make a simple loop on the head pin so it is immediately above the size 11°. Note: The loop must be large enough to fit around the size 14°s added in Step 6. Suspend the dangle from the size 14° loop at the bottom of the earring.

For the three-drop earring shown, make 3 crystal dangles. For one of the dangles place the loop ⅜" (1 cm) from the top of the crystal. Suspend the dangles from the size 14° loop at the bottom of the earring with the longer dangle placed between the shorter ones.

**Step 10:** Repeat Steps 1–9 to make the second earring.

*With the support of her husband and four children, Minnesotan Joanie Jenniges shares her passion for beadwork through designing and teaching. She can be reached at joaniejenniges@comcast.net or www.beadworkdesigns.com.*

# Montana Chandeliers

*Melody MacDuffee*

Keeping the colors subtle on this variation of the classic chandelier earring allows its graceful, elongated shape and sensuous drape to take center stage. The heavy filigree connectors add a hint of the exotic.

## Materials

- 2 g size 11° royal or Montana blue seed beads
- 18 tubular 4 × 6mm light green serpentine beads
- 10 tubular 4 × 6mm dark olive serpentine beads
- 14 oval 3 × 5mm turquoise beads
- 14 bicone 4mm Montana blue Swarovski crystal beads
- 2 bicone 6mm Montana blue Swarovski crystal beads
- 44 daisy 4mm gold-tone pewter spacers
- 20 gold head pins
- 22-gauge gold wire
- 2 gold one-to-three connectors
- 2 gold two-to-seven connectors
- 2 gold-filled earring wires

## Notions

- Chain-nose pliers
- Round-nose pliers
- Wire cutters

*Step 1:* Use head pins to make the dangles for the bottom of the earring. Each dangle corresponds to a loop on the large connector.

For the first and seventh dangles string 1 seed bead, 1 light green, 1 spacer, one 4mm crystal, 1 spacer, and 1 seed bead.

For the second and sixth dangles string 1 seed bead, 1 light green, 1 spacer, one 4mm crystal, 1 spacer, 1 oval, and 1 seed bead.

For the third and fifth dangles string 1 seed bead, 1 light green, 1 spacer, one 4mm crystal, 1 spacer, 1 oval, 1 spacer, 1 dark green, and one seed bead.

For the fourth (center) dangle string 1 seed bead, 1 light green, 1 spacer, one 4mm crystal, 1 spacer, 1 oval, 1 spacer, 1 dark green, 1 spacer, 1 light green, and 1 seed bead.

**Step 2:** Connect the dangles to the loops on the large connector. Do so by making a wrapped loop on each head pin that captures the corresponding connector loop within the dangle's loop.

**Step 3:** Use the gold wire to make a wrapped loop that captures the first loop of the small connector within the wrapped loop. String 1 oval, 1 spacer, 1 dark green, and 1 seed bead. Snug the beads and make a wrapped loop to secure them; the loop should capture the first of the two top loops on the large connector. Repeat this step for the third loop of the small connector and the second loop of the large connector.

**Step 4:** Use a head pin to string one 6mm crystal, 1 spacer, 1 light green, 1 spacer, and 1 dark green. Make a wrapped loop that captures the second (center) loop on the small connector within the wrapped loop.

**Step 5:** Attach the top loop of the small connector to an earring wire.

**Step 6:** Repeat Steps 1–5 to make the second earring.

*Melody MacDuffee has been making jewelry for many years, at first exclusively with crochet, and then gradually expanding her love of her tiny hooks and beads to a love of equally tiny beading needles and lengths of wire. She is widely published in bead and crochet publications and teaches classes a variety of techniques.*

# Jill's Earrings

*Jean Campbell*

These earrings were designed for a special Parisian sculptor. They feature two-holed Sleeping Beauty turquoise, a bead that may be difficult to find. If so, substitute any semiprecious or glass two-holed beads.

## Materials

8 rectangular 7mm × 9mm two-holed faceted beads
4 round 2mm sterling silver beads
36 sterling silver 1mm crimp tubes
4 sterling silver 3" (7.5 cm) head pins
2 sterling silver earring posts

## Notions

Round-nose pliers
Chain-nose pliers
Wire cutters

**Step 1:** String 1 round bead on each of two head pins. Pass the head pins through the holes of 1 turquoise. String 6 crimp tubes on each head pin. *Pass the head pins through the holes of 1 turquoise. String 1 crimp tube on each head pin. Repeat from * twice so you have 4 turquoise in all.

**Step 2:** Use a chain-nose pliers to gently bend the head pins together so they cross at the top of the last crimp tube (Figure 1).

Figure 1

**Step 3:** Bend the wire at the cross-point so the wires are parallel again and make a Y (Figure 2).

**Step 4:** Coil the right wire up the left wire for two coils and trim the excess.

**Step 5:** Make a wrapped loop with the left wire so it meets the coil made in Step 4.

**Step 6:** Attach an earring finding to the loop created in Step 5.

**Step 7:** Repeat all steps to make a second earring.

*Jean Campbell is the founding editor of Beadwork magazine.*

Figure 2

# Czech Cab Earrings

*Doris Coghill*

Tiny cabochons are the perfect centerpieces for these embroidered earrings. When the designer found the vintage cabs during a trip to the Czech Republic, she knew they were destined for her ears.

## Materials

Two 5 × 8mm cabochons
2 g size 15° seed beads (A)
1 g size 15° seed beads (B)
1 g size 15° seed beads (C)
2 pieces of 1½" × 1½" felt
2 pieces of 1" × 1" Ultrasuede
2 earring wires
Size D Nymo thread in color to complement beads
Silicone-based glue

## Notions

Size 12 needles
Scissors

**Step 1:** Use glue to attach one cabochon to the middle of a piece of felt. Don't let the glue leak past the edges of the cabochon or your needle will not be able to pierce the felt where there is dry glue.

**Step 2:** Tie a knot at the end of 1 yd (91.5 cm) of thread. Take a small stitch under the cabochon on the back side of the felt. Bring the thread up through the felt as close to the edge of the cabochon as possible.

**Step 3:** Work backstitch embroidery around the cabochon. Round 1: String 3 A. Push the beads down the thread so they are touching the felt and lying along the edge of the cab. Pass down through the felt at the end of the third bead. Pass back up through the felt between the first and second bead and through the second and third bead (Figure 1). This is back-stitched embroidery. Repeat around the cab.

Figure 1

For the last stitch in each round, string as many beads as needed to fit in the space to complete that round. Pass back through all beads in this round to make them line up neatly. Pass down through the felt and back up next to the completed round of beads in order to start the next round.

**Round 2:** Work backstitch using B beads.

**Round 3:** Work backstitch using C beads. When the round is completed, pass through the felt. Take a small stitch on the back to anchor the thread. Tie an overhand knot but do not cut the thread.

**Step 4:** Trim the felt even with the edge of the last row of beads, being careful not to cut your working thread or the threads on the back of the felt.

**Step 5:** Use glue to attach the trimmed piece to a piece of suede. Exit the working thread from between the two layers. Allow the glue to set for approximately 30 minutes, and then trim the piece of suede the same size as the felt.

## EDGING

**Step 6:** Take a small stitch through the suede and the felt very close to the edge, moving from back to front. Before pulling the loop of thread tight, pass the needle through the loop to form an overhand knot.

**Step 7:** String 3 A. Working from back to front, pass the needle through both layers about one bead's width from the knot. Pass up through the last bead strung (Figure 2).

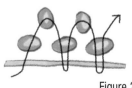

Figure 2

**Step 8:** String 2 A. Working from back to front, pass the needle through both layers about one bead's width from the last bead anchored. Pass back up through the last bead strung. The beads touching the fabric should be sitting side by side with their edges touching. Repeat around the perimeter of the earring.

**Step 9:** To finish the round of edging, string 1 A and pass down through the first bead strung in Step 7. Take another small stitch to anchor the edging. Tie an overhand knot.

**Step 10:** Find the three edging beads located at the center top of the earring. Weave through the beads and exit from either the left or right bead of the edging stitch. String 2 A, the ear wire, and 2 A. Skipping the center edging bead, go through the next one (Figure 3).

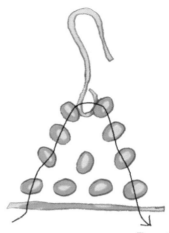

Figure 3

**Step 11:** To secure the hanging loop, pass the needle through the two layers of fabric at the edge of the earring and back up into the beads just added. Repeat at least twice more to strengthen the loop.

**Step 12:** Pass between the layers of fabric and exit between any two rounds of bead embroidery. Tie an overhand knot. Bury the end of the thread between the layers and trim.

**Step 13:** Repeat Steps 1–12 for the second earring.

*Doris Coghill left the corporate world several years ago to pursue beading full time. She teaches and designs kits (see them at www.beadsbydee.com).*

# Lampwork Dangles

*Barb Lippert*

Coming up with a fabulous pair of earrings is easier than you might guess—just find a pair of lampworked beads you can't resist and add a few beads to support and highlight them. This elegant pair of earrings was inspired by special beads found at a local bead shop. The dangles add motion and echo the colors of the focal bead.

## Materials

- 2 lampworked 12mm round beads
- 4 black 6° seed beads
- 4 Padparadscha 6mm Swarovski crystals
- 2 faceted black 4mm oval beads
- 2 sterling silver 2mm seamless ball beads
- 1 pair sterling silver angular ear wires
- 4 sterling silver 1½" (3.8 cm) head pins
- 2 sterling silver 1½" (3.8 cm) eye pins
- 2 sterling silver earring wires

## Notions

- Side cutter
- Chain-nose pliers
- Round-nose pliers

**Step 1:** String 1 oval bead and 1 silver ball on one head pin. Use the round-nose pliers to make a simple loop at the top of the head pin.

**Step 2:** Cut ½" (1.3 cm) off the top of a second head pin and string 1 crystal and 1 seed bead. Make a simple loop at the top of the head pin.

**Step 3:** Open the loop of one eye pin just wide enough to string the dangles created in Steps 1 and 2. Close the loop.

**Step 4:** String the lampworked bead, 1 crystal, and 1 seed bead on the eye pin from Step 3. Make a simple loop that touches the top of the seed bead. Trim the excess wire.

**Step 5:** Open the loop on one earring wire and string the dangle's top loop through. Close the loop.

**Step 6:** Repeat Steps 1–5 to make the second earring.

---

*Barb Lippert holds a silversmithing degree, but since she discovered beads, she's been a bit preoccupied with them. Barb and her designs currently attend art fairs, and she exhibits jewelry at several shops in the Minneapolis/St. Paul area. Barb can be reached at lips6@comcast.net.*

# Sheer Dangles

*Heidi Presteen*

Wondering what to do with leftover beads? These earrings will inspire mixes and matches that make an enchanting pair of drop earrings.

## Materials

- 16 semiprecious stone chip beads
- 34 small accent beads
- 16 thin sterling silver eye pins
- 34 thin sterling silver head pins
- 2 sterling silver earring wires

## Notions

- Round-nose pliers
- Chain-nose pliers
- Flush cutter

**Step 1:** *Use an eye pin to string 1 chip. Make a simple loop to secure the chip and trim the excess wire. Repeat from * seven times to make 8 connectors.

**Step 2:** Open one of the loops on a connector made in Step 1. Attach it to an earring wire and close the loop. *Open a loop on a second connector and attach it to the bottom of the connector just added. Close the loop. Repeat from * seven times to make a chain of 8 connectors. Set aside.

**Step 3:** *Use a head pin to string 1 accent bead. Make a simple loop to secure the bead; trim the excess wire. Repeat from * sixteen times to make 17 dangles.

**Step 4:** Use a chain-nose pliers to open the loop on one of the dangles. Attach the 3 dangles to the bottom loop on the chain made in Step 2. Continue to add the dangles to the connector chain, adding 1 dangle to each loop on the chain.

**Step 5:** Repeat Steps 1–5 to make the second earring.

*Heidi's favorite beads are crystals and pearls. She also enjoys hunting for crafty treasures, golfing, and summer weather.*

# Embellished Drop Hoops

*Sharon Bateman*

This challenging project incorporates three different stitches. Follow the thread paths in the figures carefully to make the stitching stress free, and you'll have a wonderfully funky pair of earrings in no time. Take a creative leap and experiment with other loop shapes.

## Materials

Magnifica cylinder beads in two colors (A and B)
Assortment of accent beads
¾" (2 cm) circular earring hoops
2 head pins
2 earring wires
Beading thread in color to complement beads

## Notions

Size 12 beading needle
Scissors
Round-nose pliers
Chain-nose pliers
Wire cutters (optional)
Wooden dowel (optional)

**Step 1:** Use a square knot to attach a 3' (91.5 cm) length of thread on the hoop. String 4 A beads, loop the thread around the hoop wire, and pass back through the fourth and third bead just strung. String 2 A, loop the thread around the wire, and pass back through the two beads just strung (Figure 1).

Figure 1

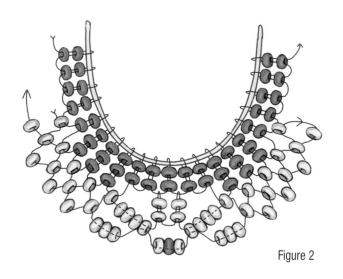

Figure 2

You are working two-bead stacks in brick stitch with the hoop as your base. Continue working around the wire from left to right, stringing A beads, looping the thread around the wire, and passing back through the bead(s) just strung. Follow the chart labeled Figure 2 (the A beads touching the hoop) for bead counts in this first round. In some cases you will be working in three-bead stacks. This step makes up your first round. *Note:* You will end up with slight gaps between the beads. Space them evenly around the hoop.

**Step 2:** You will now work right to left around the hoop. *Note:* The two-bead stacks will be counted as first, second, third, etc., from this side around. Square-stitch the first two sets of beads together to stabilize them. Weave through the beads so that you exit from the fourth two-bead stack.

**Step 3:** Work a picot edging off of the stacks. Begin by stringing 1 B, passing through the loop between the fourth and fifth stacks, and back through the bead just strung. *String 2 B, pass through the loop

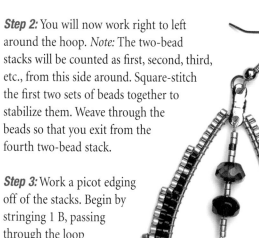

between the next two stacks, and back through the last bead just strung. Repeat from * three times. String 6 B, skip one loop, pass through the loop between the next two stacks, and back through the last two beads just strung. Repeat this step in reverse to weave the other side of the earring (Figure 2).

**Step 4:** Now work left to right around the hoop in peyote stitch. *Note:* The picot edging "point" beads will be counted as first, second, third, etc., from this side around. String 1 B and pass through the first point bead. *String 1 B and pass through the next point bead. Repeat from * twice. String 3 B and pass through the fourth point bead of the next picot. String 1 B, 1 A, 1 B, and pass through the first point bead of the next picot. String 3 B and pass through the point bead of the next picot. *String 1 B and pass through the next point bead. Repeat from * three times (Figure 2).

**Step 5:** Weave through all beads to reinforce the work. Don't pull the thread too tight or the beadwork will curl. Work gently over the gaps. If they bother you, stitch a bead between them. Knot the thread between the beads, pass through a few more, and trim the thread.

**Step 6:** If you wish, add a dangle to the center of the hoop. Begin by using a head pin to string an assortment of accent beads that will fit pleasingly in the center of the hoop. Make a wrapped loop to secure them and set the dangle aside.

String seed beads and/or accent beads along the hoop until you can add the dangle. The accent beads should hold the dangle in place.

**Step 7:** Repeat Steps 1–6 for the second earring.

*Sharon Bateman is the author of the book* Findings and Finishings *(Interweave Press, 2003). Contact her at www.sharonbateman.com.*

# Sparkly Studs

*Jean Campbell*

If you like to wear your earrings close to the lobe, try this design. They are quick to make, and it's fun to experiment with different bead colors.

## Materials

- Size 11° seed beads
- 12 size 8° triangle beads
- Size B Nymo beading thread in color to complement beads
- Two 8 mm earring posts with flat faces for gluing
- E-6000 adhesive

## Notions

- Size 12 beading or sharps needle
- Scissors
- Toothpick

**Step 1:** Create a beaded dome with circular peyote stitch.

**Round 1:** Using 2' (61 cm) of thread and leaving a 4" (10 cm) tail, string 3 seed beads. Tie a knot to make a circle. Pass through the first bead of the circle to hide the knot.

**Round 2:** String 1 seed bead and pass through the second seed bead added in Step 1. String 1 seed bead and pass through the third seed bead added in Step 1. String 1 seed bead and pass through the first seed bead added in Step 1 and the first seed bead added in this round.

**Round 3:** *String 1 triangle and pass through the next seed bead added in the previous round. Repeat from * around to add 3 triangles in all (Figure 1). Exit from the first triangle added in this round.

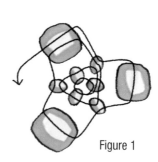

Figure 1

**Round 4:** *String 2 seed beads and pass through the next triangle added in the previous round. Repeat from * around to add 6 seed beads in all (Figure 2). Exit from the next triangle added in the previous round.

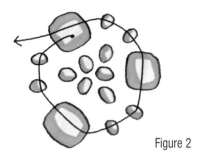

Figure 2

**Round 5:** *String 1 triangle and pass through the next triangle from Round 3. Repeat from * around to add 3 triangles in all. Exit from the first triangle added in this round.

**Round 6:** *String 3 seed beads and pass through the next triangle added in the previous round. Repeat from * around to add 9 seed beads in all (Figure 3). *Note:* The beadwork will begin to cup into a dome. Weave through all the beads in the piece again to tighten and reinforce. Pass through the first 3 seed beads strung in this round and the next triangle.

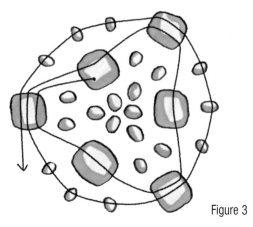

Figure 3

**Round 7:** *String 5 seed beads and pass through the next triangle added in Round 5. Repeat from * around to add 15 seed beads in all (Figure 4). *Note:* The beads added in this round will frame the beads added in Round 6.

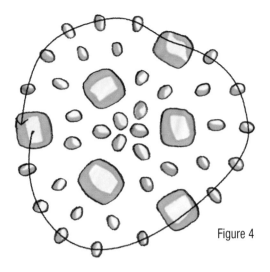

Figure 4

Weave through all the beads added in this round again, tie a knot between beads, pass through a few more beads to hide the knot, and trim close to the work. Weave the tail thread into the beadwork.

**Step 2:** Use a toothpick to apply glue to the inside/back of the dome, taking care not to let the glue ooze out to Round 7. Attach the dome to the earring finding.

**Step 3:** Repeat Steps 1–2 to make a second earring.

*Jean Campbell is the founding editor of* Beadwork *magazine.*

# Beaded Bead Stiletto

*Melody MacDuffee*

Suggesting a highly refined look, these stilettos nevertheless pack a wallop as they draw the eye from the ear down to the main event—a beaded bead as dazzling and colorful as you want it to be.

## Materials

- 16 size 11° Japanese silver-lined seed beads
- 2 round 12mm clear beads
- 92 round 3mm smoky green AB fire-polished beads
- 52 round 3mm clear silver-lined fire-polished beads
- Two 3–4" (7.5–10-cm) lengths of 2mm rounded sterling silver chain
- 2 sterling silver head pins
- 2 sterling silver earring posts
- Size B white Nymo thread

## Notions

- Size 12 beading needle
- Round-nose pliers
- Wire cutters
- Flat-nose pliers (optional)

**Step 1:** Thread a needle with 3' (91.5 cm) of thread, leaving a 6" (15 cm) tail.

**Step 2:** String 1 seed bead, 1 green bead, 1 silver-lined bead, 2 green beads, 1 silver-lined bead, 1 green bead, and 1 seed bead. This is your first strand of the first section. Pass down through a 12mm bead and through the rest of the beads just strung to attach the strand to the large bead.

**Step 3:** Pass down through the 12mm bead and through the first seed bead strung in Step 1. String 1 green, 1 silver-lined, 2 green, 1 silver-lined, and 1 green. This is your second strand of the first section. Pass through the last seed bead strung in Step 1 (Figure 1).

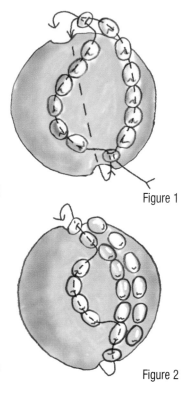

Figure 1

**Step 4:** Pass down through the 12mm and through the first seed bead of the first strand. Pass through the first green bead of the second strand. String 1 silver-lined, 2 green, and 1 silver-lined. Pass through the last green bead on the second strand and the last seed bead on the first strand (Figure 2). This is your third strand of the first section. Pass through the last seed bead strung in Step 1 (Figure 2).

Figure 2

**Step 5:** Repeat Steps 2–4 three times to make a total of four sections.

**Step 6:** If the beads don't completely cover the base bead, add another one or two strands like the third strand to fill the gap.

**Step 7:** Use a head pin to string a green bead and the beaded bead. Incorporating the bottom link of one length of chain, make a wrapped loop with the other end of the wire. Connect the ear post to the other end of the chain.

**Step 8:** Repeat Steps 1–6 to make a second earring.

---

*Melody MacDuffee has been making jewelry for many years, at first exclusively with crochet, and then gradually expanding her love of her tiny hooks and beads to a love of equally tiny beading needles and lengths of wire. She is widely published in bead and crochet publications and teaches classes a variety of techniques.*

# Deep Blue Vintage Drops

*Anna Tollin*

Do you encounter beautiful vintage crystals at your bead shop or at bead shows and shy away because you don't know what to do with them? Here's an idea: showcase them on your ears for everyone to see.

## Materials

- 2 top-drilled vintage crystal flowers
- 2 round 8mm multicolored rhinestone-embedded beads
- 2 sterling silver 8mm spacers
- 22-gauge silver wire
- 2 sterling silver earring wires

## Notions

- Chain-nose pliers
- Round-nose pliers
- Side cutter

**Step 1:** Cut an 8" (20.5 cm) piece of wire. String a vintage crystal flower and move it to the center of the wire. Bend each wire end up to make a U, with the crystal flower at the bottom of the curve. Continue bending the wire ends until they cross (Figure 1).

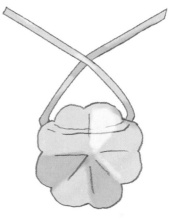

Figure 1

**Step 2:** Using a chain-nose pliers, bend the end of the right wire at the intersection until it points straight up, away from the crystal. Wrap the left wire around the right, to make a three-wrap coil (Figure 2). Cut the excess wire from the left wire end.

**Step 3:** String 1 silver bead and the rhinestone bead on the remaining wire end. Make a wrapped loop to secure the beads. Cut the excess wire.

**Step 4:** Attach the dangle to an earring wire.

Figure 2

**Step 5:** Repeat Steps 1–4 for the second earring.

---

*Anna Tollin left corporate America to pursue a more creative and authentic life. She works at The Bead Monkey in Minneapolis and will do almost anything for chocolate!*

# Crystal Dangles

*Kat Reaney*

Who said earrings have to be hard to make to be gorgeous enough to show off? You can put this pair together in a matter of minutes. So don't waste time: get it together!

## Materials

    10 crystal 10mm two-hole spacers with vertical drill holes
    8 oval 5 × 7 mm sterling silver jump rings
    2 sterling silver head pins with 2 mm silver dangles
    2 sterling silver earring wires, posts, or lever backs

## Notions

    Chain-nose pliers
    Round-nose pliers
    Wire cutters

*Step 1:* Use the chain-nose pliers to open one jump ring. Pass the jump ring through a hole in each of two spacers. Close the jump ring to connect the two spacers. *Open another jump ring. Pass it through the second hole on the last spacer strung and through a hole on another spacer. Repeat from * until you've connected five spacers.

*Step 2:* Connect one end of the spacer chain created in Step 1 to an earring finding.

*Step 3:* Use the chain-nose pliers to make a ninety-degree bend in the head pin 1mm from the bottom. Make a wrapped loop that captures the open hole of the spacer chain within the wrapped loop.

*Step 4:* Repeat all steps for the second earring.

---

*Kat Reaney works in beads, lives in beads, and dreams in beads. She and her mom have been making jewelry together for eight years. Now she works at a bead shop with many wonderful, crazy people.*

# Stardust Earrings

*Linda Richmond*

Create these dazzling earrings using ladder and herringbone stitch in the round. They're fun to make—and even more fun to wear on a starry evening.

## Materials

> Size 11° seed beads in two colors (A and B)
> 32 faceted 3mm fire polished beads (C)
> 32 faceted 3mm fire polished beads (D)
> Size B beading thread in color to complement beads
> 2 earring wires
> Beeswax or synthetic beeswax

## Notions

> Size 12 beading needle
> Chain-nose pliers

**Step 1:** Using 1 yd (91.5 cm) of doubled, waxed thread and leaving a 6" (15 cm) tail, string 2 A beads. Pass through the first bead strung again and manipulate the beads so that they sit side by side. String 1 A. Pass through the bead your tail is exiting and the bead just strung. Continue working this ladder stitch until you've joined 16 A beads. Complete the row by connecting the first and last beads added to make a circle. This is your foundation circle.

**Step 2:** Using A beads, work a round of herringbone stitch off the foundation created in Step 1. Do so by stringing 2 beads, passing down through the corresponding bead on the

Figure 1

81

foundation and up through the next foundation bead. Continue working herringbone stitch around the foundation, holding the beadwork flat (Figure 1).

Eventually the initial circle of beads will flatten out. Exit up through the first bead added in this round.

**Step 3:** String 1 C, 1 B, and 1 C. Pass down through the next bead stitched in Step 2, as you would for herringbone stitch. String 1 B and pass up through the next bead stitched in Step 2 (Figure 2). Repeat this step around the circle. Exit up through the first fire-polished bead added in this round.

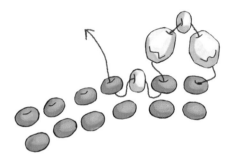

Figure 2

**Step 4:** String 1 D, 1 B, and 1 D. Pass down through the next fire-polished bead stitched in Step 3. String 1 B and pass up through the next fire-polished bead stitched in Step 3 (Figure 3). Repeat this step around the circle. Exit up through the first fire-polished and seed beads added in this round.

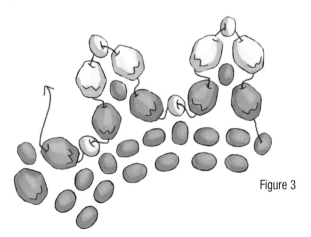

Figure 3

**Step 5:** String 4 B. Pass through the last seed bead added in Step 4 again to make a loop. Weave through these 5 beads again to secure them, then through several beads in the body of the beadwork; tie knots between beads if desired and trim the thread. Weave in and secure the tail. Attach the earring wire to the loop just made.

**Step 6:** Repeat Steps 1–5 to make a second earring.

---

*Linda Richmond of Sandpoint, Idaho, has been captivated by beads for most of her life, and she turned her passion for jewelry design into a full-time career in 1995. She sells her beadwork kits, along with beads, tools, books, and supplies, through her website at www.lindarichmond.com.*

# Shooting Stars

*Betcey Ventrella*

If you know how to work flat peyote stitch, you'll be able to make these unique earrings. Put them on and let the celestial show begin!

## Materials

- 5 g opaque black Delica beads (DB-010)
- 2 g 24K bright gold Delica beads (DB-031)
- 2 g garnet gold-luster Delica beads (DB-105)
- 24 size 2 bright gold bugle beads
- 24 bicone 4mm aurum gold 2X Swarovski crystals
- 24–30 round 3mm aurum gold 2X Swarovski crystals
- 24–30 round 3mm Siam satin Swarovski crystals
- 2 gold-filled ear wires
- 2 gold-filled bead caps
- Two 1' lengths of 2 mm twisted cotton burgundy cord
- Size B burgundy Nymo beading thread
- Fray Check
- Hypo Cement
- Masking or clear tape

## Notions

- Size 12 beading needle
- Scissors

**Step 1:** Fold the cord in half. Tape the cord together near the fold (Figure 1). Add Fray Check to the cord ends and let dry. Set aside.

**Step 2:** Following the chart (Figure 2), make a flat peyote-stitched rectangle 20 beads wide by 12 beads long.

Figure 1

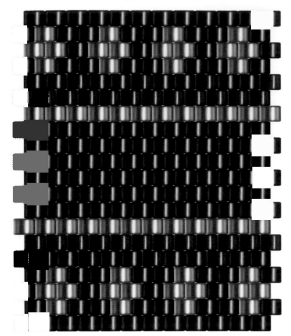

Figure 2

**Step 3:** Fold the beadwork made in Step 2 over the taped area on the cording. Bring the first and last rows of the beadwork together like a zipper to make a tube. Weave the beads together to secure the tube. Carefully insert the glue applicator between the cord and the beadwork. Apply enough glue to attach the beadwork firmly to the cord. Let dry.

**Step 4:** Following the chart (Figure 3), make two flat peyote-stitched rectangles 15 beads wide by 6 beads long.

**Step 5:** Fold one of the pieces of beadwork made in Step 4 over one end of the cording. Bring the first and last rows of the beadwork together like a zipper to make a tube. Weave the beads together to secure the tube. Carefully insert the glue applicator between the

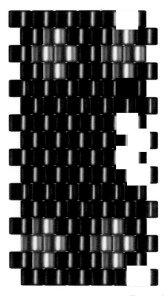

Figure 3

cord and the beadwork. Apply enough glue to attach the beadwork firmly to the cord. Let dry. Repeat this step for the remaining cord end.

**Step 6:** Weave to the bottom of one beaded tube (the side farthest away from the cord fold). String 5 black Delicas, 1 garnet Delica, 1 bugle, 1 garnet Delica, 1 round Siam crystal, 1 garnet Delica, 1 round gold crystal, and 1 garnet Delica. Skipping the last bead strung, pass back through all the beads and up through the last bead exited on the tube. Pass down through an adjacent bead at the end of the tube. Continue around to make a fringe leg for each bead at the bottom of the tube. Follow Figure 4 to make the pattern seen here or create a design of your own.

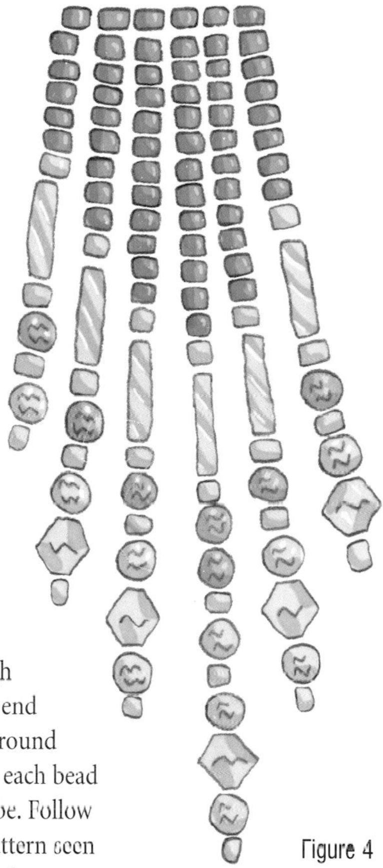

Figure 4

**Step 7:** Repeat Steps 4–6 for the other cord end.

**Step 8:** Secure a knotted thread to the top of the folded cord. Pass through 1 bead cap, 1 round Siam crystal and the loop of an earwire. Follow this thread path several times to reinforce, and tie a knot to secure.

**Step 9:** Repeat all the steps to make a second earring.

*Betcey Ventrella is the all-knowing goddess of Beyond Beadery in Rollinsville, Colorado. Contact her at Betcey@beyondbeadery.com; www.beyondbeadery.com.*

# Dipsy Doodles

*Dawn Tomlinson*

Start with a foundation and add elements to make these textured freeform earrings. The ultimate design is up to you—a chance to load up on color, use leftovers, and be daring!

## Materials

Size 14°, 11°, 8°, 6° seed beads and Delicas

Assortment of 6mm or smaller accent beads (Czech pressed glass, squares, drops, rounds, bugles, rondelles, crystals, stone chips, etc.)

8mm lampworked or other beads

2 earring wires

Silamide beading thread

## Notions

Size 10 or 12 beading needle

Scissors

Round-nose pliers

**Step 1:** String a tension bead halfway down a 1 yd length of thread. String 13 Delicas using a varied or mono-colored palette.

**Step 2:** Work in peyote stitch, following your color scheme, until your beadwork is 5 or 6 beads wide. This is the foundation for your earring.

**Step 3:** Weave to the top of the foundation and string 5 size 14°s. Pass back down into the bead next to the one you last exited. Pass through all again to secure and reinforce the circle. This will serve as your earring wire loop.

**Step 4:** Embellish the foundation with freeform stitching. Mix and match your beads to complement the foundation palette, and then choose the following techniques as you wish to complete your earring.

***Edge additions:*** Weave to the edge of the foundation and work peyote stitch with an accent bead, or work very small fringe legs from these edge beads (Figure 1).

***Wings:*** Weave to the edge of the foundation and string an odd number of size 14°s. Pass through a bead at the middle of the foundation, making sure the "wing" curves, showing no thread. Work peyote stitch off of the strand for two or three rows. To add texture, work the second and third rows with larger seed beads (Figure 2).

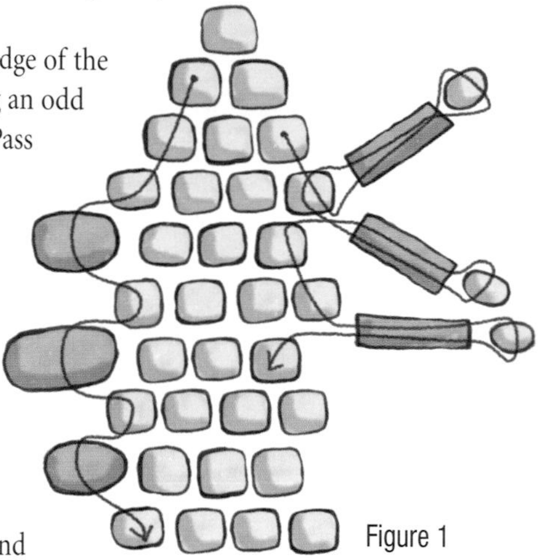

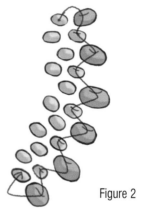

Figure 1

***Loops:*** Exiting a foundation bead, string 3 size 14°s, 1 accent bead, and 3 size 14°s. Pass back through the foundation bead to make a loop. Loops can be added at the edge, across the foundation, or over other embellishments to create depth.

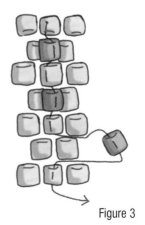

Figure 2

***Surface beads:*** Weave to an empty spot on the foundation. String 1 accent bead (rondelles work especially well for this) and 1 size 14°. Pass back through the accent bead and through the next Delica on the foundation. Pull tight.

***3-D Delicas:*** Weave to an empty spot on the foundation. String 1 Delica, move down two rows on the foundation, and pass through a corresponding bead

Figure 3

to the one you last exited (Figure 3). Repeat for at least 3 beads for good visual effect.

**Trails:** Work a two-bead wide, 7-bead long peyote-stitched strip off the edge of the foundation. Create a loop at the bottom of the strip that incorporates a drop bead (Figure 4).

**Dangles:** Weave to the bottom of the foundation. String 1 or more seed beads, 1 large bead, and at least 1 more seed bead. Skip the last bead strung and pass back through the rest. Vary the beads as you wish along the dangle.

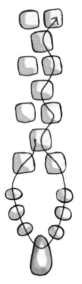

Figure 4

**Step 5:** Attach the earring finding.

**Step 6:** Make a second earring that matches the first; or choose to make one that complements the shape, color, or beads of the first.

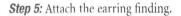

*Dawn Tomlinson has played with fibers her whole life, but finds beading and lampworking the most fun she's ever had. Born in Korea, she now lives in Eagan, Minnesota, and can be contacted at bcadartist101@msn.com.*

# Not-So-Basic Brick-Stitched Earrings

*Betcey Ventrella*

This earring design has been the gateway to the wonders of off-loom beadwork for many bead artists. The pattern is an old standby gone wild, with its long fringe featuring flashing crystals and leaves.

## Materials

Size 9° or 10° Czech three-cut seed beads in black, homatite, and aqua luster
18 dark aqua satin 25mm bugle beads
18 aqua vitrial 7 × 12mm leaf beads
14 round 3mm comet argent light 2X Swarovski crystals
18 round 4mm jet AB Swarovski crystals
6 bicone 4mm capri blue Swarovski crystals
18 oval 6 × 4mm jet AB Czech fire-polished beads
10 oval 7 × 5mm jet AB Czech fire-polished beads
2 sterling silver ear wires
Size B black Nymo beading thread

## Notions

Size 12 beading or sharps needle
Scissors

**Step 1:** Using 3' of thread and leaving a 4" tail, work a length of ladder stitch 9 beads long in this color order: 3 black, 1 aqua, 1 hematite, 1 aqua, and 3 black. Weave through all the beads again to reinforce the stitching. This will be your foundation row.

**Step 2:** Use seed beads to work decreasing brick stitch off the foundation row. You'll end up with a triangle shape.
Row 1: String 1 black and pass under the loop between the last

two beads added on the foundation row. Pass up through the bead just strung to seat it on the foundation row. Continue working brick stitch across the foundation row so the color order of the entire row is 2 black, 1 aqua, 2 hematite, 1 aqua, 2 black.

**Row 2:** Work brick stitch in this color order: 1 black, 1 aqua, 1 hematite, 1 aqua, 1 hematite, 1 aqua, and 1 black.

**Row 3:** Work brick stitch in this color order: 1 aqua, 1 hematite, 2 aqua, 1 hematite, 1 aqua.

**Row 4:** Work brick stitch in this color order: 1 hematite, 3 aqua, 1 hematite.

**Row 5:** Work brick stitch with 4 aqua.

**Row 6:** Work brick stitch in this color order: 1 aqua, 1 black, 1 aqua.

**Row 7:** Work brick stitch with 2 black.

**Step 3:** Exiting the last black added in Row 7, string 6 black seed beads and pass down through the first black added in Row 7. Repeat the thread path twice to reinforce the loop.

**Step 4:** Weave through the beads and exit down through the first bead of the foundation row. Make fringe legs across the row.

**Leg 1:** String 1 hematite, 1 bugle, 1 hematite, 1 aqua, 1 round 4mm crystal, 1 aqua, 1 small oval, 1 aqua, 3 hematite, 1 leaf, and 3 hematite.

*Pass back through the last aqua seed bead strung and up through the rest of the beads on the strand. Pass up through the foundation last exited and down through the adjacent bead.*

**Leg 2:** String 3 hematite, 1 bugle, 1 hematite, 1 aqua, 1 round 4mm crystal, 1 aqua, 1 round 3mm crystal, 1 aqua, 1 small oval, 1 aqua, 3 hematite, 1 leaf, and 3 hematite. Repeat from * to *.

**Leg 3:** String 6 hematite, 1 bugle, 1 hematite, 1 aqua, 1 round 4mm crystal, 1 aqua, 1 round 3mm crystal, 1 aqua, 1 small oval, 1 aqua, 1 large oval, 1 aqua, 3 hematite, 1 leaf, and 3 hematite. Repeat from * to *.

gle, 1 hematite, 1 aqua, 1 mm crystal, 1 aqua, 1 atite, 1 bicone crystal, 1 d 3 hematite. Repeat

**Leg 5:** String 3 hematite, 3 aqua, 6 hematite, 1 bugle, 1 hematite, 1 aqua, 1 round 4mm crystal, 1 aqua, 1 round 3mm crystal, 1 aqua, 1 small oval, 1 aqua, 1 large oval, 1 hematite, 1 round 3mm crystal, 1 bicone crystal, 1 round 3mm crystal, 1 hematite, 1 aqua, 3 hematite, 1 leaf, and 3 hematite. Repeat from * to *.

**Legs 6–9:** Repeat Legs 1–4 in reverse order.

**Step 5:** Weave from the last leg into the body of the earring, tie a knot between beads, pass through several more to hide the knot, and trim close to the work.

**Step 6:** Attach an ear wire to the loop made in Step 3.

**Step 7:** Repeat all steps to make a second earring.

*Betcey Ventrella is the all-knowing goddess of Beyond Beadery in Rollinsville, Colorado. Contact her at Betcey@beyondbeadery.com; www.beyondbeadery.com.*

# Seed Pods

*Dulcey Heller*

Here's a pair of herringbone stitch earrings you can wear with flair! At 1¼" (3.2 cm) long, their attractive shape is a flattering length for just about anyone.

## Materials

Size 10° Czech or size 11° Japanese seed beads in two colors (A and B)
Size 15° or 11° Japanese seed beads (C)
2 size 8° seed beads
2 sterling silver 3" (7.5 cm) headpins
2 sterling silver earring wires or posts
Beading thread in color to complement beads
Beeswax or synthetic beeswax

## Notions

Beading needle
Scissors
Flat- or chain-nose pliers
Round-nose pliers
Flush cutters

**Step 1:** Using 5' (152.5 cm) of thread and leaving a 6" (15 cm) tail, string 4 A. Work two stacks of beads by passing through the first 2 beads strung. String 2 A and pass through the third and fourth beads strung. This is ladder stitch. Continue using A beads to make a ladder 2 beads wide and 6 beads long, always passing down through the last two beads strung. Exit down through the last stack of beads (Figure 1).

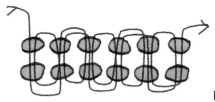

Figure 1

**Step 2:** Make a circle of beads by passing up through the first stack created in Step 1. Pass down through the last stack made in Step 1 and up through the first stack. This is your foundation circle for herringbone stitch.

**Step 3:** Make the first round of herringbone stitch. Look at the foundation circle with the holes facing up and count the beads 1–6 (Figure 2). String 2 A and pass down through the second bead in the foundation circle. Pass up through the third bead. String 2 A and pass down through the fourth bead in the foundation circle and up through the fifth bead. String 2 A and pass down through the sixth bead. Step up for the second round by passing up through the first bead in the foundation circle and through the first bead added in this step. *Note:* The beads in this round should tilt toward one another (Figure 3).

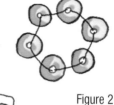

Figure 2

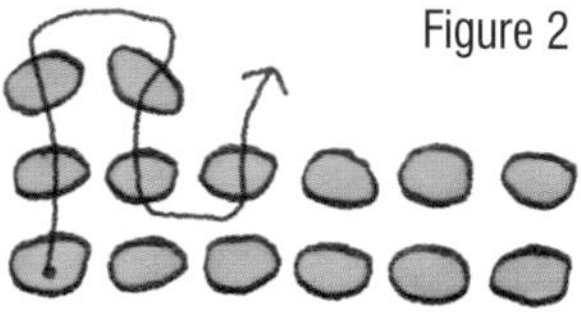

Figure 3

> **TIP**
> If you are having problems seeing the step-up to the next round, put 6 A beads in a pile. When you've stitched those 6 beads you will know it's time to step up.

**Step 4:** Make a second round of herringbone stitch. String 2 A and pass down through the second bead and up through the third bead added in Step 3. String 2 A and pass down through the fourth bead and up through the fifth bead added in Step 3. String 2 A and pass down through the sixth bead and up through the first bead added in Step 3 and the first bead added in this step.

**Step 5:** String 2 A and pass down through the second bead added in the last step. String 1 C. Pass up through the third bead added in the last step. String 2 A and pass down through the fourth bead added in the last step.

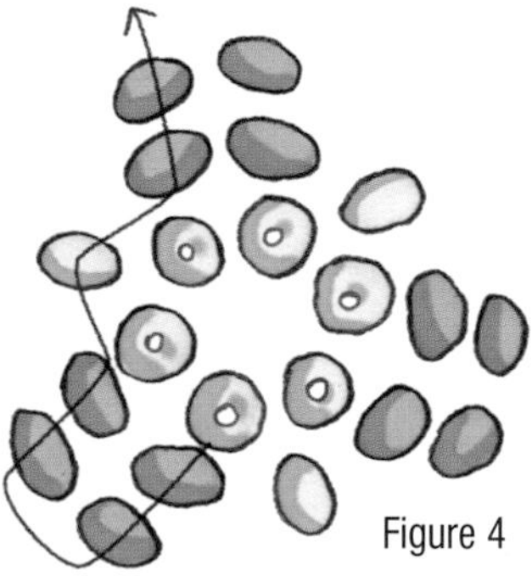

Figure 4

String 1 C. Pass up through the fifth bead added in the last step. String 2 A and pass down through the sixth bead added in the last step. String 1 C. Pass up through the first bead added in the last step and the first bead added in this step (Figure 4).

**Step 6:** Repeat Step 5, but string 2 C between each herringbone-stitched pair.

**Step 7:** Repeat Step 5, but string 3 C between each herringbone-stitched pair.

**Step 8:** Repeat Step 5, but string 4 C between each herringbone-stitched pair.

**Step 9:** Repeat Step 5, but string 5 C between each herringbone-stitched pair.

**Steps 10–12:** Repeat Step 5, but string 6 C between each herringbone-stitched pair.

**Step 13:** Repeat Step 5, but string 4 C between each herringbone-stitched pair. Keep the tension tight so that no thread is showing while you decrease the number of C beads.

**Step 14:** Repeat Step 5, but string 2 C between each herringbone-stitched pair.

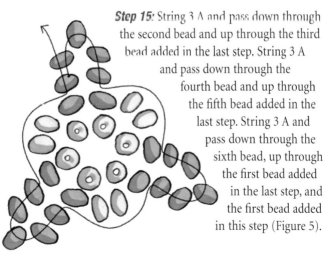

**Step 15:** String 3 A and pass down through the second bead and up through the third bead added in the last step. String 3 A and pass down through the fourth bead and up through the fifth bead added in the last step. String 3 A and pass down through the sixth bead, up through the first bead added in the last step, and the first bead added in this step (Figure 5).

Figure 5

**Step 16:** Pass down through the third bead added in the last step and up through the fourth. Pass down through the sixth bead added in the last step and up through the seventh. Pass down through the ninth bead added in the last step, up through the first bead added in the last step, and the first two beads added in this step. You now have 3 picot beads at the end of the herringbone-stitched tube. Pass through those 3 picot beads to close the tube (Figure 6).

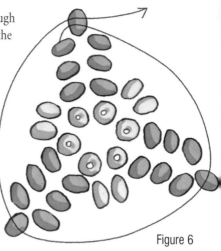

Figure 6

**Step 17:** In this step you will add picot beads to the C beads. The picots are created by pulling the C beads away from the herringbone base. *Note:* Do not poke the needle tip into the holes of the C beads or hook the thread between the beads to pull them out. Doing so damages the thread, and the piece may fall apart. Instead, poke your needle tip underneath the C beads to coax them out. There are eight picots on each panel of C beads. Count them as you work to make sure that you have pulled out and included all the rounds of C beads.

Weave through the last two rounds and pass through one of the C beads. String 1 A, 1 B, and 1 A. Loop the working thread around the thread between the second and third C beads in the next round. Pass back through the last A strung in this step (Figure 7).

**Step 18:** String 1 B and 1 A. Loop the working thread around the thread between the third and fourth beads in the next round. Pass back through the last A strung in this step.

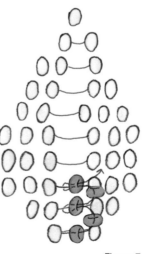

Figure 7

**Step 19:** String 1 B and 1 A. Loop the working thread around the thread between the third and fourth beads in the next round. Pass back through the last A strung in this step.

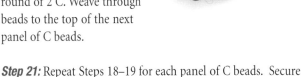

**Step 20:** Continue adding picots for each round. In the rounds that have 3 C and 5 C, choose one side of center to anchor the picot. To make the last picot, string 1 B and 1 A. Pass through 1 C in the last round of 2 C. Weave through beads to the top of the next panel of C beads.

**Step 21:** Repeat Steps 18–19 for each panel of C beads. Secure the working and tail threads and trim.

**Step 22:** Put the beadwork on a head pin. If necessary, gently straighten the headpin by pulling it between your fingers. String the beadwork (small end first) and 1 size 8°.

**Step 23:** Use round- and flat- or chain-nosed pliers to make a wrapped loop to secure the beadwork against the size 8°.

**Step 24:** Repeat Steps 1–23 to create a second earring. Attach each dangle to an earring finding.

---

*Dulcey Heller lives and beads in Minneapolis, Minnesota. She is a designer for Buy the Kit (www.buythekit.com).*

# Briolette Earring Jackets

*Chris Prussing*

Here's a way to use beads to perk up a pair of gemstone or pearl stud earrings. Just add the "jacket" to the stud before you put them on. The mesmerizing way that crystals emerge from a rocky matrix was the inspiration for this pair of line earrings.

## Materials

Size 11° crystal/black-striped Czech seed beads
Size 12° gold-lustered hex-cut Japanese seed beads
Size 15° gold-lustered Japanese seed beads
Two 10 × 7mm cut lead crystal briolettes
4 yds of 8 lb test moss green PowerPro line
2 gold-filled or 14k soldered 4.5mm round jump rings
Masking tape

## Notions

2 size 12 beading needles
Sharp scissors
Thread burner (for trimming ends)
Optivisor or other type of magnifier (optional)

**Step 1:** Fold 2 yds of line in half. Pass the fold through the middle of a jump ring, and back over the jump ring. Pull the pair of tails to tighten the fold to make a lark's head knot around the jump ring (Figure 1).

Figure 1

**Step 2:** Attach a needle to each end of the line, leaving 8" tails on each end.

**Step 3:** Work a vertical row of 13 units of two-needle right angle weave, following the pattern of alternating diagonal stripes of the size 11° and larger cut beads (Figure 2). Tack the jump-ringed end down with a bit of masking tape to hold the row in place as you work.

**Step 4:** Make the last unit of the row by stringing 1 size 11° and 4 size 15°s on the left needle. Pass through the first size 15° just strung again and string a cut bead. Use the right needle to cross back through the cut bead last strung. This step creates a picot of size 15°s at the end of the row.

**Step 5:** On the left needle string 1 briolette and 2 size 11°s. Cross the right thread back through the last bead strung.

**Step 6:** Rotate the beadwork to match Figure 3. Pass the right thread back through the adjacent cut bead from Step 4. String 4 size 15°s. Pass through the last size 15° strung again. Pass through the 2 size 11°s from Step 5 again.

**Step 7:** Work the row upward, making alternating diagonal stripes. For the final unit, pass through the adjacent size 11° of Row 1, string 2 cut beads, and cross the other thread through the last cut bead.

**Step 8:** Rotate the beadwork to match Figure 4. This row will be the front of the earring jacket. Because gemstone studs often flare outward from front to back, this row starts with 2 size 15° beads in order to make the jacket front short enough to fit against the stud. String 2 size 15°s beads, 1 size 11°, and 1 cut bead. Cross the other thread through the cut bead.

**Step 9:** Work the row upward, making alternating diagonal stripes. Create the 4-bead picot at the end by passing through the adjacent size 11° on Row 2. String 4 size 15°s and pass through the first size 15° just strung again. String 1 cut bead and cross the other thread through the cut bead just strung.

Figure 2

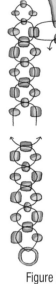

Figure 3

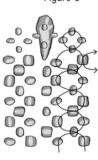

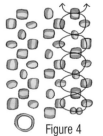

Figure 4

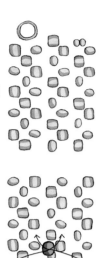

**Step 10:** Rotate the beadwork and flip it over to match Figure 5; the threads should emerge from the cut bead on the lower right side. This row zips together the edges of Rows 1 and 3. Pass the lower thread through the briolette, up through the size 11° bead on the opposite side (Row 1), and string a size 11° bead. Cross the other thread through the last bead strung. Tighten carefully to curl the edges of the work upward.

Create the final 4-bead picot by passing one thread back through the seed beads of the previous unit as in Step 6.

Figure 5

**Step 11:** Continue to zip up the jacket by following Figure 6. After the final unit, pass one thread through the beads at the top of the jacket, through the jump ring, and down through the bead on the corner of the back side. Pass the other thread through the jump ring, down through the bead on the near corner of the back side, and through the top middle bead of the back side. Tie a square knot and pass one end back through the middle bead to hide the knot. Weave through the beads downward and tie knots inside the middle beads of the next two units. Use the thread burner to invisibly trim the ends.

**Step 12:** Repeat all steps to make the second earring jacket. *Note:* To create a reverse spiral in the second jacket, follow the pattern for the first jacket, only flip the work over before you create the picot at the base of Row 2. Then flip the work back again to match the diagram and continue as for the first jacket. The briolette will appear to rest atop the picot at the base of Row 2. Do not flip the work over at the start of Row 4. The threads will emerge from the cut bead at the lower left of the work. Proceed as in Step 10, but pass the lower thread through the briolette from left to right instead.

Figure 6

*Chris Prussing owns a bead shop in Juneau, Alaska, and is the author of* Beading with Right Angle Weave *(Interweave Press, 2004).*

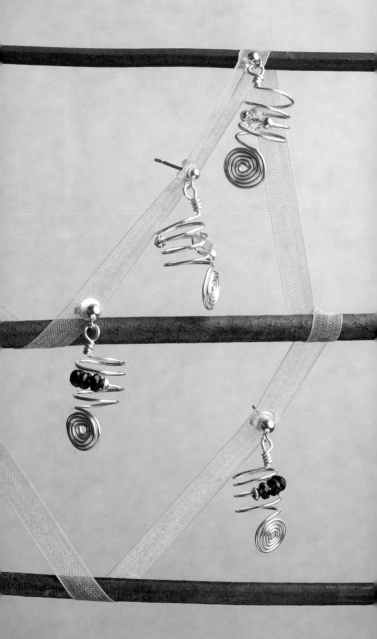

# Coiling Points

Anne Cox

These attractive wireworked earrings combine three
techniques every beginner knows—wrapped loops, coils,
and spirals. Change the number of coils, the size of the
spiral, or the number of beads to create a different look.

## Materials

Assortment of rondelle 2 × 4mm (or smaller) beads
2 sterling silver earring posts
18-gauge silver wire
Hypo Cement

## Notions

Round-nose pliers
Chain-nose pliers
12mm diameter dowel (or marker)
Wire cutters

**Step 1:** Make a wrapped loop at the end of approximately 8"
of wire.

**Step 2:** Hold the loop securely against the dowel in a parallel
direction. Work left to right to make 3–5 coils (Figure 1).

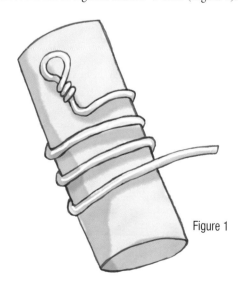

Figure 1

**Step 3:** String the desired amount of beads on the coil. The beads can slide loose along the coil, but if you'd like to affix them to the wire, carefully apply glue to the bead holes with the needle applicator.

**Step 4:** Work a spiral with the remaining wire end.

**Step 5:** Manipulate the wire so the coils are evenly spaced and the spiral sits neatly beneath the coil. Attach the dangle to the earring finding.

**Step 6:** Repeat all steps to make a second earring, this time wrapping the coil (Step 2) from left to right.

---

*Anne Cox is a Colorado dodgeball beader—one who dives between work, family, and friends to find time to bead.*

# Flowerette Tassels

Barb Grainger

Tassels are everywhere these days, and they're especially nice for body adornment. These earrings take fringe a step higher with an elegant flowerette technique. Make variations by changing the number, size, or shape of focal beads, or using a bead cap instead of a bead.

## Materials

Size 11° seed beads
2 faceted 10mm glass beads
2 faceted 6mm glass beads
2 earring wires
Silamide thread
Beeswax or synthetic beeswax

## Notions

Size 12 beading needle or sharps
Scissors

**Step 1:** Using 1 yd of waxed thread and leaving a 6" tail, string 4 size 11°s. Pass through all the beads again, exiting from the fourth bead. Manipulate the beads until they form a square. String one 6mm and one 10mm.

**Step 2:** String 31 size 11°s. This is your base strand. Skip the last 3 beads strung and pass through the next 4 beads on the strand. * String 3 seed beads, pass up through the bead the thread is exiting from and 3 of the strand beads (Figure 1). Repeat from * five times. Pass through the remaining size 11°, the 2 large faceted beads, the loop created in Step 1, and back through the 2 large faceted beads.

**Step 3:** Repeat Step 2 four times.

**Step 4:** Weave down into one of the fringe legs. Tie a knot between beads if desired, pass through a few beads, and trim the thread close to the work. Repeat with the thread tail.

**Step 5:** Add an earring wire to the loop at the top of the earring.

Figure 1

**Step 6:** Repeat all steps to make a second earring.

*Author, instructor, and designer, Barb Grainger is also a frequent contributor to* Beadwork *magazine. Contact her at beadteach@aol.com*

# Techniques

### STARTING A NEW THREAD

There's no doubt that you'll run out of thread as you work on your necklaces that use off-loom stitches. It's easy to begin a new thread. There are a couple of solutions. I prefer the first way because it's stronger.

*Solution 1:* Tie off your old thread when it's about 4" long by making a simple knot between beads. Pass through a few beads and pull tight to hide the knot. Weave through a few more beads and trim the thread close to the work. Start the new thread by tying a knot between beads and weaving through a few beads. Pull tight to hide the knot. Weave through several beads until you reach the place to begin again.

*Solution 2:* Here's how to end your old thread without tying a knot. Weave the thread in and out, around and around, through several beads and then trim it close to the work. Begin a new thread the same way, weaving the end of the thread in and out, around and around, and through several beads until you reach the place to begin again.

### PASS THROUGH VS. PASS BACK THROUGH

Pass through means to move your needle in the same direction as the beads have been strung. Pass back through means to move your needle in the opposite direction.

### TENSION BEAD

A tension bead holds your work in place. To make one, string a bead larger than those you are working with, then pass through the bead again, making sure not to split your thread. The bead will be able to slide along, but will still provide tension to work against.

## Wirework

### Simple loops

To make a simple loop, grasp one end of
the wire with round-nose pliers. Holding
on to the wire with one hand, gently turn
the pliers until the wire end and wire body
touch. Create a 90 degree reverse bend
where they meet.

### Wire-wrapped loops

For a wire-wrapped
loop, cut the desired
length of wire and
make a 90 degree bend
2" from one end. Use round-nose
pliers to hold the wire near the
angle and bend the short end up
and around the pliers until it meets
itself. Wrap the wire tightly down the
neck of the wire to create a couple of
coils. Trim the excess to finish.

### Coil

To make a coil, use one hand to hold the end of your
wire against a mandrel. With the other hand, wrap the wire
around the mandrel in tight loops. To
remove the coil, slide it off the mandrel
and cut. Add vertical loops on either
end to use the coil as is, or cut the coil
at certain intervals to make jump rings
or split rings.

### Spiral

To start a spiral, make a small loop
at the end of a wire with round-
nose pliers. Enlarge the piece by
holding on to the spiral with
chain-nose pliers and pushing the
wire over the previous coil with
your thumb.

### Netting (single thread)

Begin by stringing a base row of 13 beads. String 5 beads and go back through the fifth bead from the end of the base row. String another 5 beads, skip 3 beads of the base row, and go back through the next. Repeat to the end of the row, passing through the fifth, fourth, and third beads of those just strung and exiting from the third. Turn the work over and go back across the same way.

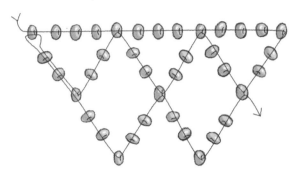

### Brick stitch

Begin by creating a foundation row in ladder stitch or using a secured thread. String one bead and pass under the closest exposed loop of the foundation row. Pass back through the same bead and continue, adding one bead at a time.

To decrease within a row, string one bead and skip a loop of thread on the previous row, passing under the second loop and back through the bead.

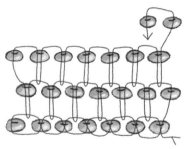

To increase within a row, work two stitches in the same space of the previous row.

### Ladder stitch

Using two needles, one threaded on each end of the thread, pass one needle through one or more beads from left to right and pass the other needle through the same beads

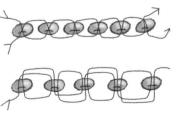

from right to left. Continue adding beads by crisscrossing both needles through one bead at a time. Use this stitch to make strings of beads or as the foundation for brick stitch.

For a single-needle ladder, string 2 beads and pass through them again. String 1 bead. Pass through the last stitched bead and the one just strung. Repeat, adding one bead at a time and working in a figure-eight pattern.

## Flat peyote stitch

One-drop peyote stitch begins by stringing an even number of beads to create the first two rows. Begin the third row by stringing one 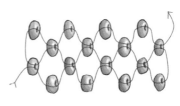 bead and passing through the second-to-last bead of the previous rows. String another bead and pass through the fourth-to-last bead of the previous rows. Continue adding one bead at a time, passing over every other bead of the previous rows.

Two-drop peyote stitch is worked the same as above, but with two beads at a time instead of one.

## Tubular peyote stitch

String an even number of beads and make a foundation circle by passing through them two more times, exiting from the first bead strung. String 1 bead and pass through the third bead of the foundation circle. String 1 bead and pass 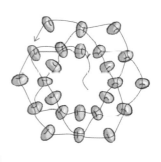 through the fifth bead of the foundation circle. Continue adding 1 bead at a time, skipping over 1 bead of the first round, until you have added half the number of beads of the first round. Exit from the first bead of the second round.

String 1 bead, pass through the second bead added in the second round, and pull thread tight. String 1 bead and pass through the third bead added in the second round. Continue around, filling in the "spaces" 1 bead at a time. Exit from the first bead added in each round.

### Single-needle right-angle weave

*The illustration refers to bead positions, not bead numbers.*

*Row 1:* String four base beads. Pass through beads in positions 1, 2, and 3. The bead in position 3 will become the bead in position 1 in the next group. String 3 beads. Pass through bead in position 3 of last group (now position 1 of this group), bead in position 2 and bead in position 3 (now position 1 of next group). String 3 beads. Continue working in this pattern until the row is to a desired length. In the last group, pass through beads in positions 1, 2, 3, and 4.

*Row 2:* String 3 beads. Pass through bead in position 4 of previous group and bead in position 1 of this group. String 2 beads. Pass through bead in position 2 of Row 1, bead in position 1 of previous group, and the beads just added. Pass through bead in position 4 of Row 1. String 2 beads. Pass through bead in position 2 of previous group and bead in position 4 of Row 1. Pass through first bead just added. String 2 beads. Pass through bead in position 2 of Row 1, bead in position 1 of previous group, and the first bead just added.

*Row 3:* Repeat Row 2.

### Right-angle weave (double needle)

Using two needles, one on each end of the thread, string three beads on one of the needles and slide them to the center of the thread. String a fourth bead, passing one needle through from left to right and passing the other needle through from right to left. String one bead with each needle, then pick up one more bead and pass one needle through from left to right and pass the other needle through from right to left. Con-

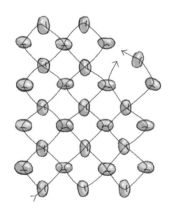

tinue for desired length of row. To work the next row, repeat as for the first row, stringing new beads only onto the right thread and passing back through beads from the first row with the left thread.

To make a row-end decrease, simply stop your row short and begin a new row.

### Flat herringbone stitch

Begin with a foundation row of even-count ladder stitch. String 2 beads, pass down through the second to last bead in the ladder, and up through the next bead. String 2 beads, pass down the next bead and then up through the following.

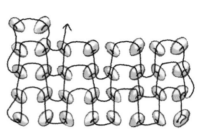

Repeat to the end of the row. To end the row, pass back through the last bead strung. To begin the next row, string 2 beads and pass down through the second to last bead of the previous row. Repeat, stringing 2 beads per stitch and passing down then up through two beads of the previous row. The 2-bead stitch will cause the beads to angle-up in each row, like a herringbone fabric.

### Tubular herringbone stitch

Begin with a foundation row of ladder stitch. Join the ends together to form a tube. String 2 beads. Pass down through the next bead and up through the bead after it. Repeat around the tube. At the end of the round, pass through the first beads of the previous and current rounds to step up to the new round.

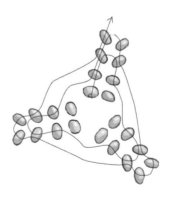

### Square stitch

Begin by stringing a row
of beads. For the second
row, string 2 beads, pass
through the second-to-
last bead of the first
row, and back through
the second bead of

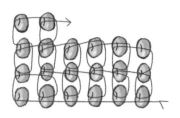

those just strung. Continue by stringing 1 bead, passing
through the third-to-last bead of the first row, and back
through the bead just strung. Repeat this looping technique to
the end of the row.

To make a decrease, weave thread through the previous row
and exit from the bead adjacent to the place you want to
decrease. Continue working in square stitch.

To make an increase, string the number of beads at the end of
the row you want to increase. Work the next row the same as
the previous row.

### Bead embroidery

For single stitch
embroidery, begin by
passing the needle
through the fabric,

from wrong side to right side, at the place where the first bead
is to go. String a bead and pass the needle back through the
fabric right next to the bead. Bring the needle back through
the fabric where the next bead is to go, thread one bead and
go back down through the fabric. Continue.

Use bugle beads between two seed beads to protect the
thread from the sharp edges on bugle beads and single-stitch
as one bead.

### Simple fringe

Exit from your foundation row of
beads or fabric. String a length of
beads plus 1 bead. Skipping the
last bead, pass back through all
the beads just strung to create a
fringe leg. Pass back into the
foundation row or fabric.

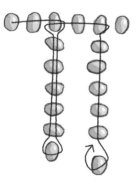

# The art and craft of
# BEADWORK

*Books dedicated to building your skills
and to fueling your creativity*

## Beadwork Creates™ Series
Edited by Jean Campbell,
founding editor of *Beadwork* magazine

Dazzle everyone with beautiful
hand-beaded bracelets, necklaces, bags, rings, and beaded
beads. Learn simple stringing,
loomwork, peyote stitch, and
other techniques as you create
stylish jewelry.

**Beadwork Creates Bracelets**
ISBN 1-931499-20-9
Paperback, $16.95

**Beadwork Creates
Necklaces**
ISBN 1-931499-22-5
Paperback, $16.95

**Beadwork Creates
Beaded Beads**
ISBN 1-931499-27-6
Paperback, $16.95

**Beadwork Creates
Beaded Bags**
ISBN 1-931499-34-9
Paperback, $16.95

**Beadwork Creates
Beaded Rings**
ISBN 1-931499-26-8
Paperback, $16.95